Aberdeenshire Library and Information Service
www.aberdeenshire.gov.uk/libraries
Renewals Hotline 01224 661511

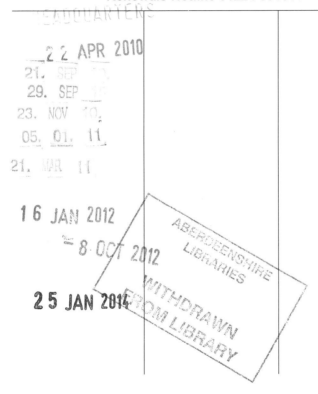

Speedy meals

641.
555

Good Housekeeping

easy to make!
Speedy Meals

COLLINS & BROWN

First published in Great Britain in 2008
by Collins & Brown
10 Southcombe Street
London W14 0RA

An imprint of Anova Books Company Ltd

The Good Housekeeping website is
www.goodhousekeeping.co.uk

10 9 8 7 6 5 4 3 2

ISBN 978-1-84340-448-4

A catalogue record for this book is available from the British
Library.

Reproduction by Dot Gradations Ltd
Printed and bound by SNP Leefung, China

Keep updated. Email food@anovabooks.com

This book can be ordered direct from the publisher. Contact the
marketing department, but try your bookshop first.

www.anovabooks.com

NOTES

- Both metric and imperial measures are given for the recipes. Follow either set of measures, not a mixture of both, as they are not interchangeable.
- All spoon measures are level.
  1 tsp = 5ml spoon; 1 tbsp = 15ml spoon.
- Ovens and grills must be preheated to the specified temperature.
- Use sea salt and freshly ground black pepper unless otherwise suggested.
- Fresh herbs should be used unless dried herbs are specified in a recipe.
- Medium eggs should be used except where otherwise specified. Free-range eggs are recommended.
- Note that certain recipes, including mayonnaise, lemon curd and some cold desserts, contain raw or lightly cooked eggs. The young, elderly, pregnant women and anyone with an immune-deficiency disease should avoid these, because of the slight risk of salmonella.
- Calorie, fat and carbohydrate counts per serving are provided for the recipes.

Picture Credits
Photographers: Craig Robertson; Nicki Dowey (pages 71, 74, 78, 79, 80, 98, 104); Lucinda Symons (pages 72 and 77)
Stylist: Helen Trent
Home economist: Mari Mererid Williams

Contents

Foreword

Getting supper on the table when you're short of time should be just as much fun as when you've several hours to spend pottering in the kitchen. That's why we've put together this book, *Speedy Meals*, which shows you how simple it is to cook a family meal in just half an hour. We have a tantalising choice of recipes, such as the healthy nutritious salads that can be thrown in a bowl so everyone can help themselves, and a moreish selection of warming soups. There are simple suppers such as our deli pizza, using time-saving ready-made ingredients that are just as good as home made, so you're not stinting on flavour. If you're looking for something more substantial, try lamb with spicy couscous, beef stroganoff, or one of our quick and easy pasta sauces. Plus we've thrown in lots of great recipes for quick puddings such as rich chocolate pots and lemon mousse.

We've gathered together 101 ideas for quick midweek suppers with the minimum of fuss. All the recipes have been triple-tested in the Good Housekeeping kitchens to make sure they work every time for you.

Emma

Emma Marsden
Cookery Editor
Good Housekeeping

0

The Basics

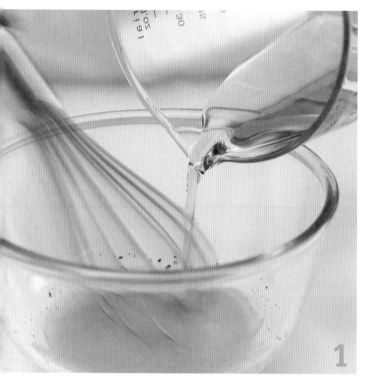

French Dressing

To make 100ml (3½ fl oz), you will need:
1 tsp Dijon mustard, a pinch of sugar, 1 tbsp red or white wine vinegar, 6 tbsp extra virgin olive oil, salt and ground black pepper.

1   Put the mustard, sugar and vinegar in a small bowl, and season with salt and pepper. Whisk until well combined, then gradually whisk in the olive oil until thoroughly combined.

2   Store in a cool place if not using immediately. Whisk briefly before using.

Variation

Garlic Dressing: add 1 crushed garlic clove to the dressing with the mustard, sugar and vinegar.

Salad dressings

There's a wonderful array of salad ingredients available these days and a tasty meal can be rustled up in no time. But while it doesn't take much effort to make a salad into a proper meal, we all need some inspiration for dressing recipes from time to time. Try these quick and easy dressings for salads with the wow factor.

Six quick salad dressings

Balsamic

Put 2 tbsp balsamic vinegar and 4 tbsp extra virgin olive oil in a small bowl and whisk to combine. Season with salt and ground black pepper.

Wholegrain Mustard

Put 1 tbsp wholegrain mustard, juice of ½ lemon and 6 tbsp extra virgin olive oil in a small bowl and whisk to combine. Season with salt and ground black pepper.

Blue Cheese Dressing

To make 150ml (5fl oz), you will need:
50g (2oz) Roquefort cheese, 2 tbsp low-fat yogurt,
1 tbsp white wine vinegar, 5 tbsp extra virgin olive oil,
salt and ground black pepper.

1 Crumble the cheese into a food processor with the
yogurt, vinegar and olive oil.

2 Whiz for 1 minute until thoroughly combined, then
season – taste before adding salt as the blue cheese
is salty. Store in a cool place and use within 24 hours.

Balsamic Mustard

Put 1–2 tbsp balsamic vinegar, 1 tsp Dijon mustard,
4 tbsp olive oil, salt and ground black pepper in a small
bowl and whisk to combine.

Lemon and Parsley

Put the juice of ½ lemon, 6 tbsp extra virgin olive oil and
4 tbsp freshly chopped flat-leafed parsley in a medium
bowl and whisk to combine. Season generously with salt
and ground black pepper.

Fresh Herb

Put ½ tsp Dijon mustard, a pinch of sugar and 1 tbsp
lemon juice in a bowl and season with salt and ground
black pepper. Whisk until well combined, then
gradually whisk in 6 tbsp extra virgin olive oil until
thoroughly combined. Stir in 2 tbsp freshly chopped
herbs, such as parsley, chervil and chives.

Dijon Mustard

Put 2 tbsp vinegar, 4 tbsp olive oil and 1½ tsp Dijon
mustard in a small bowl and whisk to combine. Season
with salt and ground black pepper.

Pasta

Perfectly cooked pasta can be a super-quick accompaniment or a meal in itself. Whether you are cooking dried or fresh pasta, follow these simple steps, then add an easy pasta sauce for a meal in minutes.

How much pasta do I need?

Allow 75g (3oz) dried pasta shapes or noodles or 125g (4oz) fresh or filled pasta shapes per person. Cook the pasta until al dente – tender, with a slight bite at the centre. Follow the timings on the pack and start testing 1 minute before the recommended time. The pasta will continue to cook a little after draining.

Cooking pasta

There are a number of mistaken ideas about cooking pasta, such as adding oil to the water, adding salt only at a certain point and rinsing the pasta after cooking. The basics couldn't be simpler. Filled pasta is the only type of pasta that needs oil in the cooking water – the oil reduces friction, which could tear the wrappers and allow the filling to come out. Use 1 tbsp for a large pan of water. Rinse pasta after cooking only if you are going to cool it to use in a salad.

Dried pasta

1   Heat the water with about 1 tsp salt per 100g (3½ oz) of pasta. Bring to a rolling boil, then add all the pasta and stir well for 30 seconds, to keep the pasta from sticking.

2   Once the water is boiling again, set the timer for 2 minutes less than the cooking time on the pack and cook uncovered.

3   Check the pasta when the timer goes off, then every 60 seconds until it is cooked al dente: tender, but with a slight bite at the centre. Drain in a colander.

Fresh pasta

Fresh pasta is cooked in the same way as dried, but for a shorter time. Bring the water to the boil. Add the pasta to the boiling water all at once and stir well. Set the timer for 2 minutes and keep testing every 30 seconds until the pasta is cooked al dente: tender, but with a little bite at the centre. Drain in a colander.

Eight quick pasta sauces

Quick and Easy Carbonara

Fry 150g (5oz) chopped smoked bacon rashers in
1 tbsp olive oil for 4–5 minutes. Add to drained,
cooked pasta, such as tagliatelle, and keep hot. Put
2 large egg yolks in a bowl, add 150ml (5fl oz) double
cream and whisk together. Add to the pasta with
50g (2oz) freshly grated Parmesan and 2 tbsp freshly
chopped parsley.

Tomato, Prawn and Garlic

Put 350g (12oz) cooked peeled prawns in a bowl with
4tbsp sun-dried tomato paste and stir well. Heat 1tbsp
olive oil and 15g (¹/₂ oz) butter in a frying pan and
gently cook 3 sliced garlic cloves until golden. Add
4 large chopped tomatoes and 125ml (4fl oz) dry white
wine. Leave the sauce to bubble for about 5 minutes,
then stir in the prawns and 20g (³/₄ oz) freshly chopped
parsley.

Creamy Pesto

Put 5 tbsp freshly grated Parmesan, 25g (1oz) toasted
pinenuts, 200g carton low-fat fromage frais and 2 garlic
cloves into a food processor. Whiz to a thick paste.
Season generously with salt and ground black pepper.
Add 40g (1¹/₂ oz) each torn fresh basil leaves and roughly
chopped fresh parsley and whiz for 2-3 seconds.

Lemon and Parmesan

Cook pasta shells in a large pan of boiling salted water
for the time stated on the pack. Add 125g (4oz) frozen
petit pois to the pasta water for the last 5 minutes of
the cooking time. Drain the pasta and peas, put back in
the pan and add the grated zest and juice of ¹/₂ lemon
and 75g (3oz) freshly grated Parmesan. Season with
ground black pepper, toss and serve immediately.

Mushroom and Cream

Heat 1 tbsp olive oil in a large pan and fry 1 finely
chopped onion for 7–10 minutes until soft. Add 300g
(11oz) sliced mushrooms and cook for 3–4 minutes.
Pour in 125ml (4fl oz) dry white wine and bubble for
1 minute, then stir in 500ml (18fl oz) low-fat crème
fraîche. Heat until bubbling, then stir in 2 tbsp freshly
chopped tarragon. Season with salt and ground black
pepper.

Courgette and Anchovy

Heat the oil from a 50g can anchovies in a frying pan.
Add 1 crushed garlic clove and a pinch of dried chilli
and cook for 1 minute. Add 400ml (14fl oz) passata,
2 diced courgettes and the anchovies. Bring to the
boil, then reduce the heat and simmer for about 10
minutes, stirring well, until the anchovies have melted.

Walnut and Creamy Blue Cheese

Heat 1 tsp olive oil in a small pan, add 1 crushed
garlic clove and 25g (1oz) toasted walnut pieces and
cook for 1 minute – the garlic should just be golden.
Add 100g (3¹/₂oz) cubed Gorgonzola and 150ml (5fl oz)
single cream. Season with ground black pepper.

Broccoli and Thyme

Put 900g (2lb) trimmed tenderstem broccoli in a pan
with 150ml (¹/₄ pint) hot vegetable stock. Bring to the
boil, then cover and simmer for 3–4 minutes until
tender – the stock should have evaporated. Add
2 crushed garlic cloves and 2 tbsp olive oil and cook
for 1–2 minutes to soften the garlic. Add 250g carton
mascarpone, 2 tbsp freshly chopped thyme and 100g
(3¹/₂ oz) freshly grated pecorino cheese and mix
together. Season with salt and ground black pepper.

Perfect pasta

Use about 1 litre (1³/₄ pints) of water per 100g
(3¹/₂oz) of pasta.
If a recipe calls for cooking the pasta with the
sauce after it has boiled, undercook the pasta slightly
when boiling it.
Rinse the pasta only if you are going to cool it to
serve as a salad, then drain well and toss with oil.

Cooking rice and potatoes

The popular staples of rice and potatoes transform meat, poultry, fish and vegetable dishes into substantial meals. Perfectly cooked rice is easy to achieve, while potatoes are one of the most versatile of all vegetables.

Perfect rice

Use 50–75g (2–3oz) raw rice per person – or measure by volume 50–75ml (2–2½fl oz).
If you cook rice often, you may want to invest in a special rice steamer. They are available in Asian supermarkets and some kitchen shops and give good, consistent results.

Cooking rice

There are two main types of rice: long-grain and short-grain. Long-grain rice is generally served as an accompaniment, while short-grain rice is used for dishes such as risotto, sushi and paella. Long-grain rice needs no special preparation, although basmati should be washed to remove excess starch.

Basmati rice

Put the rice in a bowl and cover with cold water. Stir until this becomes cloudy, then drain and repeat until the water is clear. Soak the rice for 30 minutes then drain before cooking.

Long-grain rice

1 Use 50–75g (2–3oz) raw rice per person; measured by volume 50–75ml (2–2½fl oz). Measure the rice by volume and put it in a pan with a pinch of salt and twice the volume of boiling water (or stock).

2 Bring to the boil. Turn the heat down to low and set the timer for the time stated on the pack. The rice should be al dente: tender with a bite at the centre.

3 When the rice is cooked, fluff up the grains with a fork.

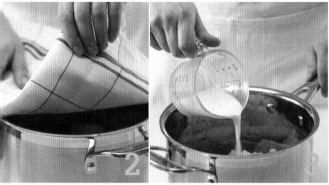

Boiling potatoes

Peel or scrub old potatoes, scrape or scrub new potatoes. Cut large potatoes into even-sized chunks and put them in a pan with plenty of salted cold water. Cover, bring to the boil, then reduce the heat and simmer until cooked – about 10 minutes for new potatoes, 15–20 minutes for old.

Mashing potatoes

To serve four, you will need:
900g (2lb) floury potatoes such as Maris Piper, 125ml (4fl oz) full-fat milk, 25g (1oz) butter, salt and ground black pepper.

1 Peel the potatoes and cut into even-sized chunks. Boil as above until just tender, 15–20 minutes. Test with a small knife. Drain well.

2 Put the potatoes back in the pan and cover with a clean teatowel for 5 minutes, or warm them over a very low heat until the moisture has evaporated.

3 Pour the milk into a small pan and bring to the boil. Pour on to the potatoes with the butter and season with salt and pepper.

4 Mash the potatoes until smooth, light and fluffy.

Making potato chips

1 Heat vegetable oil in a deep-fryer to 160°C (test by frying a small cube of bread; it should brown in 60 seconds). Cut potatoes into chips and dry on kitchen paper. Fry in batches for 6–7 minutes until soft. Drain on kitchen paper.

2 Turn up the heat and heat the oil to 190°C (a cube of bread will brown in 20 seconds). Fry the chips until golden brown. Drain well, sprinkle with salt and serve immediately.

Perfect mash

To mash vegetables you can use a mouli-légumes, a potato masher or a ricer. The mouli and ricer give the smoothest results.
Mashing is also suitable for parsnips, sweet potatoes and celeriac.

Stir-frying

Stir-fries can be as simple or as substantial as you feel like making them. And if you buy ready-prepared stir-fry vegetables, a meal can be on the table in minutes. Ensure your wok or pan is very hot before you start cooking and keep the ingredients moving.

Stir-frying vegetables

Stir-frying is perfect with non-starchy vegetables, as the quick cooking preserves their colour, freshness and texture.

To serve four, you will need:
450g (1lb) vegetables, 1–2 tbsp vegetable oil, 2 crushed garlic cloves, 2 tbsp soy sauce, 2 tsp sesame oil.

1 Cut the vegetables into even-sized pieces. Heat the vegetable oil in a large wok or frying pan until smoking-hot. Add the garlic and cook for a few seconds, then remove and set aside.

2 Add the vegetables to the wok, and toss and stir them. Keep them moving constantly as they cook, which will take 4–5 minutes.

3 When the vegetables are just tender, but still with a slight bite, turn off the heat. Put the garlic back into the wok and stir well. Add the soy sauce and sesame oil, toss and serve.

Perfect stir-frying

Cut everything into small pieces of uniform size so that they cook quickly and evenly.
If you're cooking onions or garlic with the vegetables, don't keep them over the high heat for too long or they will burn.
Add liquids towards the end of cooking so that they don't evaporate.

Stir-frying fish

Choose a firm fish such as monkfish, as more delicate fish will break up.

1 Cut into bite-sized pieces. Heat a wok or large pan until very hot and add oil to coat the inside.

2 Add the fish and toss over a high heat for 2 minutes until just cooked. Remove to a bowl. Cook the other ingredients you are using for the stir-fry. Return the fish to the wok or pan for 1 minute to heat through.

Stir-frying poultry and meat

Stir-frying is ideal for poultry and tender cuts of meat.

1 Trim off any fat, then cut the poultry or meat into even-sized strips or dice no more than 5mm (¼ in) thick. Heat a wok or large pan until hot and add oil to coat the inside.

2 Add the poultry or meat and cook, stirring constantly, until just done. Remove to a bowl. Cook the other ingredients you are using for the stir-fry, then return the poultry or meat to the pan and cook for 1–2 minutes to heat through.

Quick sauces, salsas and butters

A simple grilled chop, steak, chicken breast or fish fillet is a quick and easy meal, but can be made even tastier with the addition of a sauce, salsa or flavoured butter.

Five quick sauces

Mustard and Caper

Mash 2 hard-boiled egg yolks with 2 tsp smooth Dijon mustard. Add 2 tbsp white wine vinegar and slowly whisk in 8 tbsp olive oil. Add 2 tbsp chopped capers, 1 tbsp finely chopped shallot and a pinch of sugar. Season well with salt and ground black pepper. Use for grilled fish, beef, pork or sausages.

Tangy Herb

Put 2 tbsp each freshly chopped flat-leafed parsley, mint and basil in a bowl, add 2 tbsp roughly chopped capers, 1 tsp Dijon mustard, 2 crushed garlic cloves, 150ml (¼ pint) olive oil and the juice of ½ lemon and combine thoroughly using a fork. Use for grilled or fried steak.

Peanut

Heat 1 tbsp vegetable oil in a pan, add 2 tbsp curry paste, 2 tbsp brown sugar and 2 tbsp peanut butter and fry for 1 minute. Add 200ml (7fl oz) coconut milk and bring to the boil, stirring all the time, then simmer for 5 minutes. Use for grilled or stir-fried chicken.

Tarragon

Put 500ml (18fl oz) crème fraîche, 1 tsp Dijon mustard and 1 crushed garlic clove in a pan. Bring to the boil and simmer for a few minutes. Add 2 tbsp freshly chopped tarragon just before serving. Use for chicken or fish.

Curried Coconut

Heat 2 tbsp extra virgin olive oil in a pan, add 175g (6oz) finely chopped onions with 1 tbsp water and cook gently for 10 minutes or until softened and golden brown. Add 2 crushed garlic cloves, 2.5cm (1in) piece fresh root ginger, peeled and grated, and 3–4 tbsp mild curry paste and cook for 1–2 minutes. Mix 3 tbsp coconut milk powder with 450ml (¾ pint) warm water, stir into the curried mixture and bring to the boil. Let it bubble for 5–10 minutes. Season with salt to taste. Use for fish or shellfish.

Five quick salsas

Quick Tomato

Put 4 roughly chopped tomatoes, $^1/_2$ ripe, peeled and roughly chopped avocado, 1 tsp olive oil and the juice of $^1/_2$ lime in a bowl and stir well. Use for grilled fish or chicken.

Smoky

Put 75g (3oz) finely chopped onions or shallots, 150ml ($^1/_4$ pint) shop-bought barbecue sauce, 100ml ($3^1/_2$fl oz) maple syrup, 1 tbsp cider vinegar, 1 tbsp soft brown sugar, 100ml ($3^1/_2$fl oz) water, 1 tsp lemon juice and a little grated lemon zest in a pan. Bring to the boil and leave to bubble for 10–15 minutes until syrupy. Take the pan off the heat and add 6 finely chopped spring onions and 175g (6oz) finely chopped fresh pineapple. Serve warm or cold. Use for burgers.

Mango and Fennel

Put 1 halved and diced mango, 1 small trimmed and diced fennel bulb, 1 seeded and finely diced chilli, 1 tbsp balsamic vinegar, 2 tbsp freshly chopped flat-leafed parsley and 2 tbsp freshly chopped mint in a bowl. Add the juice of 1 lime, stir to combine and season generously with salt and ground black pepper. Use for grilled chicken.

Avocado, Tomato and Coriander

Put 1 chopped red onion in a bowl and add 1 ripe, peeled and chopped avocado, 4 large roughly chopped tomatoes, a small handful of roughly chopped fresh coriander and the juice of 1 lime. Mix well, then season with salt and ground black pepper. Use at once for grilled pork chops or chicken.

Prawn and Avocado

Put 2 large ripe, peeled and roughly chopped avocados in a large bowl, then add 350g (12oz) cooked, peeled king prawns, 6 small finely sliced spring onions, 3 tbsp freshly chopped coriander, the grated zest and juice of 3 limes and 8 tbsp olive oil. Mix well, then season with salt and ground black pepper. Use for smoked salmon or grilled fish.

Flavoured butter

You will need:
25g (1oz) soft unsalted butter per serving, plus flavouring (see below).

1 Beat the softened butter together with the flavouring. Turn out on to clingfilm, shape into a log, and wrap tightly. Chill in the refrigerator for at least 1 hour. Keep for up to one week (or freeze for up to one month.)

2 To serve, slice the log into pieces about 5mm ($^1/_4$ in) thick and use for freshly grilled fish, chicken, meat or vegetables.

Flavourings

For 125g (4oz) unsalted butter.
Anchovy Butter: 6 mashed anchovy fillets.
Herb Butter: 2 tbsp finely chopped fresh herbs, a squeeze of lemon juice.
Garlic Butter: 1 crushed garlic clove, 2 tsp finely chopped fresh parsley.

Preparing eggs

There are only three essentials to basic egg preparation: cracking, separating and whisking – and once you have mastered these simple techniques you will be able to cook eggs in lots of different ways.

Cracking and separating

You'll need to separate eggs for making sauces such as mayonnaise, soufflés, meringues and some cakes. It's easy, but it requires care. If you're separating more than one egg, break each one into an individual cup. Separating them individually means that if you break one yolk, you won't spoil the whole batch. Keeping the whites yolk-free is particularly important for techniques such as whisking.

1 Crack the egg more carefully than usual: right in the middle to make a break between the two halves that is just wide enough to get your thumbnail into.

2 Holding the egg over a bowl with the large end pointing down, carefully lift off the small half. Some of the white will drip and slide into the bowl while the yolk sits in the large end of the shell.

3 Carefully slide the yolk into the smaller end, then back into the large end to allow the remaining white to drop into the bowl. Take care not to break the yolk; even a speck can stop the whites from whisking up.

How can I tell if my eggs are fresh?

A fresh egg should feel heavy in your hand and will sink to the bottom of the bowl or float on its side when put into water (1).
Older eggs, over two weeks old, will float vertically (2).

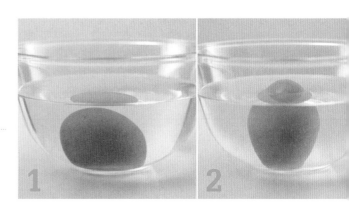

Whisking

1 Use an electric mixer or hand whisk. Make sure that there is no trace of yolk in the whites and that the whisk and bowl are clean and dry. At a low speed, use the whisk in a small area of the whites until it starts to become foamy.

2 Increase the speed and work the whisk through the whites until glossy and soft rounded peaks form. Do not over-whisk as the foam will become dry and grainy.

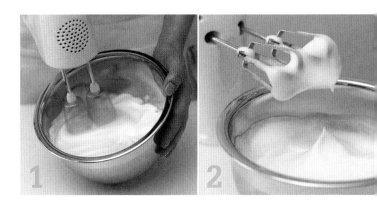

Making omelettes

There are numerous different types of omelette – from the classic folded omelette made from simple beaten eggs to thick omelettes such as Spanish tortilla and Italian frittata.

Classic omelette

To serve one, you will need: 2 eggs, 15g (½oz) butter, salt and ground black pepper.

1 Heat a heavy-based 18cm (7in) frying pan or omelette pan. Using a fork, beat the eggs and seasoning. Add the butter to the pan and let it sizzle for a few moments without browning, then pour in the eggs and stir a few times with a fork.

2 As the omelette begins to stick at the sides of the pan, lift it up and let the uncooked egg run into the gap.

3 When the omelette is nearly set and the underneath is brown, loosen the edges and give the pan a sharp shake to slide the omelette across.

4 Add a filling (such as grated cheese or fried mushrooms) if you like, and fold the far side of the omelette towards you. Tilt the pan to slide the omelette on to the plate and serve.

Perfect omelettes

Use a high heat. **Beat** the eggs lightly.
Don't add butter until the pan is already hot, otherwise it will brown too much.

Preparing vegetables

Onions and shallots have a pungent taste that becomes milder when they are cooked, and are often used as a basic flavouring for savoury dishes. Garlic and chillies are stronger flavouring ingredients. Tomatoes and peppers add depth and richness to a variety of dishes. All of these frequently used vegetables can be quickly prepared.

Onions

1 Cut off the tip and base of the onion. Peel away all the layers of papery skin and any discoloured layers underneath.

2 Put the onion root end down on the chopping board, then, using a sharp knife, cut the onion in half from tip to base.

3 **Slicing** Put one half on the board with the cut surface facing down and slice across the onion.

4 **Chopping** Slice the halved onions from the root end to the top at regular intervals. Next, make two or three horizontal slices through the onion, then slice vertically across the width.

Cook's Tips

When you want a meal in a hurry, take advantage of the time-saving ingredients available and buy:
• Packs of chopped root vegetables
• Packs of chopped stir-fry vegetables
• Prepared cauliflower and broccoli florets
• Ready-prepared chips
• Bags of washed and prepared salad
• Frozen broad beans and peas
• Frozen chopped fresh herbs
• Ready-made garlic paste
• Roasted vegetables in oil, such as red peppers, artichokes and sunblush or sun-dried tomatoes

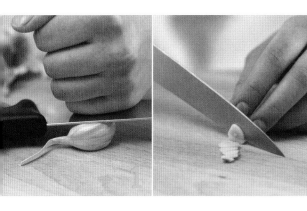

Garlic

1. Put the clove on a chopping board and place the flat side of a large knife on top of it. Press down firmly on the flat of the blade to crush the clove and break the papery skin.

2. Cut off the base of the clove and slip the garlic out of its skin. It should come away easily.

3. **Slicing** Using a rocking motion with the knife tip on the board, slice the garlic as thinly as you need.

4. **Shredding and chopping** Holding the slices together, shred them across the slices. Chop the shreds if you need chopped garlic.

5. **Crushing** After step 2, the whole clove can be put into a garlic press. To crush with a knife: roughly chop the peeled cloves with a pinch of salt.

6. **Puréeing** Press down hard with the edge of a large knife tip (with the blade facing away from you), then drag the blade along the garlic while still pressing hard. Continue to do this, dragging the knife tip over the garlic.

Chillies

1. Cut off the cap and slit open lengthways. Using a spoon, scrape out the seeds and the pith.

2. For diced chilli, cut into thin shreds lengthways, then cut crossways.

Cook's Tip

Wash hands thoroughly after handling chillies – the volatile oils will sting if accidentally rubbed into your eyes.

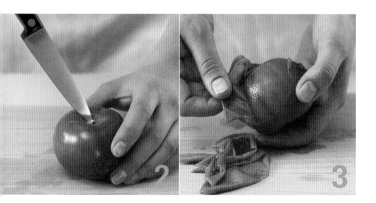

Peeling tomatoes

1 Fill a bowl or pan with boiling water. Using a slotted spoon, add the tomato for 15–30 seconds, then remove to a chopping board.

2 Use a small sharp knife to cut out the core in a single cone-shaped piece. Discard the core.

3 Peel off the skin; it should come away easily, depending on ripeness.

Seeding tomatoes

1 Halve the tomato through the core. Use a small sharp knife or a spoon to remove the seeds and juice. Shake off the excess liquid.

2 Chop the tomato as required for your recipe and place in a colander for a minute or two, to drain off any excess liquid.

Seeding peppers

1 Cut the pepper in half vertically and snap out the white pithy core and seeds. Trim away the rest of the white membrane with a knife.

2 Alternatively, cut off the top of the pepper then cut away and discard the seeds and white pith.

Cook's Tip

The seeds and white pith of peppers taste bitter so should be removed before you use the peppers. Some people find pepper skins hard to digest. To peel raw peppers, use a swivel-handled peeler to cut off strips down the length of the pepper. Use a small knife to cut out any parts of skin that the peeler could not reach. Alternatively, chargrilling whole peppers gives them a smoky flavour and makes them easier to peel (see below).

Chargrilling peppers

1 Hold the pepper, using tongs, over the gas flame on your hob (or under a preheated grill) until the skin blackens all over.

2 Put in a bowl, cover and leave to cool (the steam will help to loosen the skin). Peel.

Segmenting citrus fruits

1 Cut off a slice at both ends of the fruit, then cut off the peel, just inside the white pith.

2 Hold the fruit over a bowl to catch the juice and cut between the segments just inside the membrane to release the flesh. Continue until all the segments are removed. Squeeze the juice from the membrane into the bowl and use as required.

Preparing fruit

A few simple techniques can make preparing both familiar and not-so-familiar fruits quick and easy.

Preparing papaya

1 If using in a salad, peel the fruit using a swivel-headed vegetable peeler, then gently cut in half using a sharp knife. Remove the shiny black seeds and fibres using a teaspoon. Slice the flesh, or cut into cubes.

2 If serving on its own, halve the fruit lengthways using a sharp knife, and remove the seeds and fibres as above.

Preparing mangoes

1 Cut a slice to one side of the stone in the centre. Repeat on the other side.

2 Cut parallel lines into the flesh of one slice, almost to the skin. Cut another set of lines to cut the flesh into squares.

3 Press on the skin side to turn the fruit inside out, so that the flesh is thrust outwards. Cut off the chunks as close as possible to the skin. Repeat with the other half.

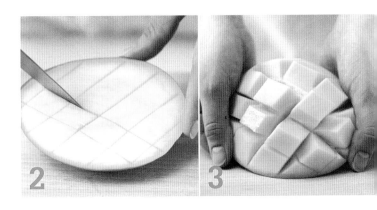

Ice creams and quick sauces

Rich and creamy, fresh and fruity or sweet and indulgent, ice creams are an ideal instant solution to how to end your meal. And with the addition of a quick and easy sauce, you can transform them into something extra special.

Instant Banana Ice Cream

To serve four, you will need:
6 ripe bananas, about 700g (1½lb), peeled, cut into thin slices and frozen (see Cook's Tip), 1–2 tbsp virtually fat-free fromage frais, 1–2 tbsp orange juice, 1 tsp vanilla extract, a splash of rum or Cointreau (optional), a few drops of lime juice to taste.

1 Leave the frozen banana to stand at room temperature for 2–3 minutes. Put the still frozen pieces in a food processor or blender with 1 tbsp fromage frais, 1 tbsp orange juice, the vanilla extract and the rum or liqueur, if you like.

2 Whiz until smooth, scraping down the sides of the bowl and adding more fromage frais and orange juice as necessary to give a creamy consistency. Add lime juice to taste and serve at once or turn into a freezer container and freeze for up to one month.

Cook's Tip

To freeze bananas, peel and slice them thinly, then put the banana slices on a large non-stick baking tray and put into the freezer for 30 minutes or until frozen. Transfer to a plastic bag and store in the freezer until needed.

Three quick sauces

The Best Chocolate Sauce

Put 75g (3oz) roughly chopped plain chocolate into a small heatproof bowl set over a pan of simmering water, making sure the bottom of the bowl doesn't touch the water. Pour in 150ml (¼ pint) double cream, then leave the chocolate to melt over very low heat. It will take about 10 minutes. Don't stir, or it will thicken to a sticky mess. Once melted, gently stir until smooth. Serve with ice cream or poached pears.

Variations

- Add a shot of espresso coffee to the cream and chocolate while they're melting together.
- Use mint-flavoured chocolate instead of plain.
- Pour a little orange or coffee-flavoured liqueur into the bowl while the chocolate and cream are melting.

Raspberry Coulis

To serve four to six, you will need:
225g (8oz) raspberries, 2 tbsp Kirsch or framboise eau de vie, icing sugar to taste.

1 Put the raspberries in a blender or food processor with the Kirsch or eau de vie. Whiz until they are completely puréed.

2 Transfer the purée to a fine sieve, and press and scrape it through the sieve until nothing is left but the dry pips.

3 Sweeten with icing sugar to taste and chill until needed.

Butterscotch

Heat 50g (2oz) butter, 50g (2oz) golden caster sugar, 75g (3oz) light muscovado sugar and 150g (5oz) golden syrup together gently, stirring, until melted. Cook for 5 minutes, then remove from the heat. Stir in 125ml (4fl oz) double cream, a few drops of vanilla extract and the juice of ½ lemon and stir over a low heat for 1–2 minutes.

Strawberry

Put 225g (8oz) hulled strawberries and 2–3 tbsp icing sugar in a food processor and whiz well to combine. Sieve the sauce and chill until needed.

Food storage and hygiene

Storing food properly and preparing it in a hygienic way is important to ensure that food remains as nutritious and flavourful as possible, and to reduce the risk of food poisoning.

Hygiene

When you are preparing food, always follow these important guidelines:

Wash your hands thoroughly before handling food and again between handling different types of food, such as raw and cooked meat and poultry. If you have any cuts or grazes on your hands, be sure to keep them covered with a waterproof plaster.

Wash down worksurfaces regularly with a mild detergent solution or multi-surface cleaner.

Use a dishwasher if available. Otherwise, wear rubber gloves for washing-up, so that the water temperature can be hotter than unprotected hands can bear. Change drying-up cloths and cleaning cloths regularly. Note that leaving dishes to drain is more hygienic than drying them with a teatowel.

Keep raw and cooked foods separate, especially meat, fish and poultry. Wash kitchen utensils in between preparing raw and cooked foods. Never put cooked or ready-to-eat foods directly on to a surface which has just had raw fish, meat or poultry on it.

Keep pets out of the kitchen if possible; or make sure they stay away from worksurfaces. Never allow animals on to worksurfaces.

Shopping

Always choose fresh ingredients in prime condition from stores and markets that have a regular turnover of stock to ensure you buy the freshest produce possible.

Make sure items are within their 'best before' or 'use by' date. (Foods with a longer shelf life have a 'best before' date; more perishable items have a 'use by' date.)

Pack frozen and chilled items in an insulated cool bag at the check-out and put them into the freezer or refrigerator as soon as you get home.

During warm weather in particular, buy perishable foods just before you return home. When packing items at the check-out, sort them according to where you will store them when you get home – the refrigerator, freezer, storecupboard, vegetable rack, fruit bowl, etc. This will make unpacking easier – and quicker.

The storecupboard

Although storecupboard ingredients will generally last a long time, correct storage is important:

Always check packaging for storage advice – even with familiar foods, because storage requirements may change if additives, sugar or salt have been reduced. Check storecupboard foods for their 'best before' or 'use by' date and do not use them if the date has passed.

Keep all food cupboards scrupulously clean and make sure food containers and packets are properly sealed.

Once opened, treat canned foods as though fresh. Always transfer the contents to a clean container, cover and keep in the refrigerator. Similarly, jars, sauce bottles and cartons should be kept chilled after opening. (Check the label for safe storage times after opening.)

Transfer dry goods such as sugar, rice and pasta to moisture-proof containers. When supplies are used up, wash the container well and thoroughly dry before refilling with new supplies.

Store oils in a dark cupboard away from any heat source as heat and light can make them turn rancid and affect their colour. For the same reason, buy olive oil in dark green bottles.

Store vinegars in a cool place; they can turn bad in a warm environment.

Store dried herbs, spices and flavourings in a cool, dark cupboard or in dark jars. Buy in small quantities as their flavour will not last indefinitely.

Store flours and sugars in airtight containers.

Refrigerator storage

Fresh food needs to be kept in the cool temperature of the refrigerator to keep it in good condition and discourage the growth of harmful bacteria. Store day-to-day perishable items, such as opened jams and jellies, mayonnaise and bottled sauces, in the refrigerator along with eggs and dairy products, fruit juices, bacon, fresh and cooked meat (on separate shelves), and salads and vegetables (except potatoes, which don't suit being stored in the cold). A refrigerator should be kept at an operating temperature of 4–5°C. It is worth investing in a refrigerator thermometer to ensure the correct temperature is maintained.

To ensure your refrigerator is functioning effectively for safe food storage, follow these guidelines:

To avoid bacterial cross-contamination, store cooked and raw foods on separate shelves, putting cooked foods on the top shelf. Ensure that all items are well wrapped.

Never put hot food into the refrigerator, as this will cause the internal temperature of the refrigerator to rise.

Avoid overfilling the refrigerator, as this restricts the circulation of air and prevents the appliance from working properly.

It can take some time for the refrigerator to return to the correct operating temperature once the door has been opened, so don't leave it open any longer than is necessary.

Clean the refrigerator regularly, using a specially formulated germicidal refrigerator cleaner. Alternatively, use a weak solution of bicarbonate of soda: 1 tbsp to 1 litre (1³/₄ pints) water.

If your refrigerator doesn't have an automatic defrost facility, defrost regularly.

Maximum refrigerator storage times

For pre-packed foods, always adhere to the 'use by' date on the packet. For other foods the following storage times should apply, providing the food is in prime condition when it goes into the refrigerator and that your refrigerator is in good working order:

Vegetables and Fruit

Green vegetables	3–4 days
Salad leaves	2–3 days
Hard and stone fruit	3–7 days
Soft fruit	1–2 days

Dairy Food

Cheese, hard	1 week
Cheese, soft	2–3 days
Eggs	1 week
Milk	4–5 days

Fish

Fish	1 day
Shellfish	1 day

Raw Meat

Bacon	7 days
Game	2 days
Joints	3 days
Minced meat	1 day
Offal	1 day
Poultry	2 days
Raw sliced meat	2 days
Sausages	3 days

Cooked Meat

Joints	3 days
Casseroles/stews	2 days
Pies	2 days
Sliced meat	2 days
Ham	2 days
Ham, vacuum-packed (or according to the instructions on the packet)	1–2 weeks

1

Healthy Salads

Tomato, Mozzarella and Red Pesto Salad

225g (8oz) baby plum tomatoes, halved
225g (8oz) baby mozzarella, drained
100g jar red pepper pesto
175g (6oz) pitted black olives, drained
100g (3½oz) mixed salad leaves
salt and ground black pepper

1 Put the tomatoes, mozzarella, pesto and olives in a large bowl and toss together. Season with pepper. Check the seasoning before adding any salt, though, as the olives are already salty. Cover the bowl and put to one side.

2 Just before serving, toss the salad leaves with the tomato and mozzarella mixture.

Cook's Tip

If you can't find baby mozzarella, buy larger buffalo mozzarella instead – available from most major supermarkets – and cut it into large cubes.

EASY

Preparation Time
10 minutes

NUTRITIONAL INFORMATION

Per Serving
400 calories, 36g fat (of which 12g saturates),
3g carbohydrate, 2.9g salt

Vegetarian • Gluten free

Serves
4

Try Something Different

Warm Duck Salad: season two 225g (8oz) duck breast fillets. Heat a frying pan, add the duck breasts, skin side down, and cook for 5 minutes. Turn and cook the other side for 5 minutes. Roast in a preheated oven, 200°C (180°C fan oven) mark 6, for 10 minutes. Complete the recipe, omitting the Quorn. Slice the duck and serve on the salad leaves.

Warm Salad with Quorn and Berries

2 tbsp olive oil

1 onion, sliced

175g pack Quorn pieces

2 tbsp raspberry vinegar

150g (5oz) blueberries

225g (8oz) mixed salad leaves

salt and ground black pepper

1 Heat the olive oil in a frying pan, add the onion and cook for 5 minutes or until soft and golden. Increase the heat and add the Quorn pieces. Cook, stirring, for 5 minutes or until golden brown. Season with salt and pepper, put into a large bowl and put to one side.

2 Add the raspberry vinegar, 75ml (3fl oz) water and the blueberries to the frying pan. Bring to the boil and bubble for 1–2 minutes until it reaches a syrupy consistency.

3 Gently toss together the Quorn mixture, blueberry mixture and salad leaves. Serve immediately.

Serves 4	EASY		NUTRITIONAL INFORMATION	
	Preparation Time 5 minutes	**Cooking Time** 12 minutes	**Per Serving** 152 calories, 7g fat (of which 1g saturates), 8g carbohydrate, 0.3g salt	Vegetarian Gluten free • Dairy free

Warm Tofu, Fennel and Bean Salad

1 tbsp olive oil, plus 1 tsp

1 red onion, finely sliced

1 fennel bulb, finely sliced

1 tbsp cider vinegar

400g can butter beans, drained and rinsed

2 tbsp freshly chopped flat-leafed parsley

200g (7oz) smoked tofu

salt and ground black pepper

1 Heat 1 tbsp olive oil in a large frying pan. Add the onion and fennel, and cook over a medium heat for 5–10 minutes until soft.

2 Add the cider vinegar and heat through for 2 minutes. Stir in the butter beans and parsley, season with salt and pepper, then tip into a bowl.

3 Slice the smoked tofu into four, then into eight triangles. Add to the pan with the remaining olive oil. Cook for 2 minutes on each side or until golden.

4 Divide the bean mixture among four plates, and add two slices of tofu to each plate.

EASY

Preparation Time	Cooking Time
10 minutes	15 minutes

NUTRITIONAL INFORMATION

Per Serving
150 calories, 6g fat (of which 1g saturates),
15g carbohydrate, 0.8g salt

Vegetarian
Gluten free • Dairy free

Serves
4

Smoked Trout, Tomato and Lemon Salad

4 ripe tomatoes, preferably vine-ripened, sliced

caster sugar to sprinkle

5 tbsp crème fraîche

2 tbsp horseradish cream

2 tbsp dill and mustard sauce

grated zest of ½ lemon and 2 tbsp lemon juice

275g (10oz) smoked trout fillets, flaked

4 thick slices country-style bread

1 Little Gem lettuce, leaves separated

salt and ground black pepper

1 thin-skinned lemon, peeled and very thinly sliced, to garnish

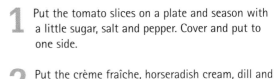

1 Put the tomato slices on a plate and season with a little sugar, salt and pepper. Cover and put to one side.

2 Put the crème fraîche, horseradish cream, dill and mustard sauce, lemon zest and juice in a large bowl. Whisk together and season with salt and pepper.

3 Add the smoked trout to the crème fraîche mixture and toss together.

4 Toast the bread lightly on both sides. Put a slice of toast on each of four serving plates. Arrange the tomato slices on the toast; spoon over any tomato juice. Arrange the lettuce and the trout mixture on top of the tomatoes, garnish with the lemon slices and serve.

Serves 4	EASY		NUTRITIONAL INFORMATION
	Preparation Time 20 minutes	**Cooking Time** 3 minutes	**Per Serving** 295 calories, 14g fat (of which 7g saturates), 20g carbohydrate, 4.3g salt

Salmon, Mango and Watercress Salad

1 ripe mango, peeled, stoned and cubed
1 small bunch of watercress, chopped
1 red onion, finely sliced
2 x 150g packs hot-smoked salmon fillets

For the orange and parsley dressing
2 tbsp extra virgin olive oil
2 tsp white wine vinegar
juice of 1 small orange
1 tbsp freshly chopped parsley
salt and ground black pepper

1 Put the mango into a large bowl with the watercress and onion.

2 In a small bowl, whisk together the olive oil, vinegar, orange juice and parsley. Season with salt and pepper, then toss the dressing through the salad.

3 Divide the salmon and salad among four plates and serve immediately.

EASY

Preparation Time
10 minutes

NUTRITIONAL INFORMATION

Per Serving
221 calories, 14g fat (of which 2g saturates),
8g carbohydrate, 0.1g salt

Gluten free • Dairy free

Serves
4

Cook's Tips

Chillies vary enormously in strength, from quite mild to blisteringly hot, depending on the type of chilli and its ripeness. Taste a small piece first to check it's not too hot for you. To prepare, see page 23.

Be extremely careful when handling chillies not to touch or rub your eyes with your fingers, as they will sting. Wash knives immediately after handling chillies for the same reason. As a precaution, use rubber gloves when preparing them if you like.

Chinese Prawn Noodle Salad

450g (1lb) straight-to-wok medium egg noodles

2 red chillies, seeded and finely chopped (see Cook's Tips)

4 spring onions, finely sliced

½ cucumber, halved lengthways, seeded and finely diced

350g (12oz) cooked king prawns

1 tbsp freshly chopped coriander

For the soy and sesame dressing

2 tbsp runny honey

2 tbsp dark soy sauce

2 tbsp rice wine vinegar

4 tbsp sesame oil

ground black pepper

1 Put the noodles into a bowl and pour over boiling water to cover. Cover the bowl with clingfilm and leave for 5 minutes.

2 To make the dressing, whisk the honey, soy sauce, vinegar and sesame oil together with some black pepper. Drain the noodles and, while still warm, pour over the dressing. Toss together, then leave to cool. If you have time, chill for 30 minutes–1 hour.

3 To serve, stir the chillies, spring onions, cucumber, prawns and coriander into the noodles, and pile into four bowls.

	EASY	NUTRITIONAL INFORMATION	
Serves **4**	**Preparation Time** 15 minutes, plus 5 minutes soaking and chilling	**Per Serving** 632 calories, 21g fat (of which 4g saturates), 88g carbohydrate, 2.2g salt	Gluten free • Dairy free

250g (9oz) cooked (vacuum-packed without vinegar) beetroot, diced

1 tbsp olive oil

2 tsp white wine vinegar

350g (12oz) potato salad

1–2 tbsp lemon juice

4 peppered smoked mackerel fillets, skinned and flaked

2 tbsp freshly chopped chives, plus extra to garnish

salt and ground black pepper

Smoked Mackerel Salad

1 Put the beetroot in a bowl. Sprinkle with the olive oil and vinegar. Season with salt and pepper, and toss together.

2 In a large bowl, mix the potato salad with the lemon juice to taste. Season with salt and pepper. Add the flaked mackerel and chopped chives and toss together.

3 Just before serving, pile the mackerel mixture into four serving bowls. Sprinkle the beetroot over the top of the salad and garnish with chives.

EASY

Preparation Time
15 minutes

NUTRITIONAL INFORMATION

Per Serving
656 calories, 56g fat (of which 10g saturates),
16g carbohydrate, 2.4g salt

Gluten free • Dairy free

Serves
4

Cherry Tomato and Salami Pasta Salad

200g (7oz) fusilli or other dried pasta shapes

150g (5oz) cherry tomatoes, halved if large

150g (5oz) baby leaf spinach

75g (3oz) pepper salami, shredded

3 tbsp black olive tapenade

3 tbsp freshly chopped chives

2 tbsp pine nuts, lightly toasted

salt and ground black pepper

1 Cook the pasta in a large pan of lightly salted boiling water according to the packet instructions. Drain, rinse under cold water, then drain well. Tip into a large bowl.

2 Add the remaining ingredients to the pasta, toss everything together, and season with black pepper. Check the seasoning before adding salt – the tapenade may have made the salad salty enough.

3 Pile the salad into a large serving bowl. If not being served straight away, this salad is best kept in a cool place, but not chilled, until needed.

Serves 4	EASY		NUTRITIONAL INFORMATION	
	Preparation Time 5 minutes	**Cooking Time** 10–15 minutes	**Per Serving** 332 calories, 20g fat (of which 6g saturates), 28g carbohydrate, 2g salt	Dairy free

Chicken with Spicy Couscous

125g (4oz) couscous

1 ripe mango, peeled, stoned and cut into 2.5cm (1in) chunks

1 tbsp lemon or lime juice

125g tub fresh tomato salsa

3 tbsp mango chutney

3 tbsp orange juice

2 tbsp freshly chopped coriander, plus extra to garnish

200g pack char-grilled chicken fillets

4 tbsp fromage frais

salt and ground black pepper

lime wedges to garnish

1 Put the couscous in a large bowl, pour over 300ml (½ pint) boiling water, season well with salt and pepper, and leave to stand for 15 minutes.

2 Put the mango chunks on a plate and sprinkle with the lemon or lime juice.

3 Mix together the tomato salsa, mango chutney, orange juice and coriander.

4 Drain the couscous if necessary, fluff the grains with a fork, then stir in the salsa mixture and check the seasoning. Turn out on to a large serving dish, and arrange the chicken and mango on top.

5 Just before serving, spoon the fromage frais over the chicken, and garnish with chopped coriander and lime wedges.

EASY

Preparation Time
15 minutes, plus
15 minutes soaking

NUTRITIONAL INFORMATION

Per Serving
187 calories, 4g fat (of which 1g saturates),
24g carbohydrate, 0.1g salt

Serves
4

Chicken Tikka with Coconut Dressing

125ml (4fl oz) crème fraîche
5 tbsp coconut milk
4 pitta breads
200g (7oz) mixed salad leaves
400g (14oz) cooked chicken tikka fillets, sliced
2 spring onions, finely sliced
2 tbsp mango chutney
15g (1/2oz) flaked almonds
25g (1oz) raisins

1 Mix the crème fraîche and coconut milk together in a bowl, and put to one side.

2 Split each pitta bread to form a pocket, then fill each pocket with a generous handful of salad leaves. Divide the chicken among the pitta breads. Sprinkle some spring onion over the chicken, add the mango chutney and drizzle with the crème fraîche mixture. Top with a sprinkling of flaked almonds and raisins. Serve immediately.

Serves 4	EASY	NUTRITIONAL INFORMATION
	Preparation Time 10 minutes	**Per Serving** 493 calories, 17g fat (of which 9g saturates), 53g carbohydrate, 1.1g salt

Throw-it-all-together Salad

2–4 char-grilled chicken breasts, torn into strips

2 carrots, peeled into strips

$1/2$ cucumber, halved lengthways, seeded and cut into ribbons

a handful of fresh coriander leaves, roughly chopped

$1/2$ head of Chinese leaves, shredded

4 handfuls of watercress

4 spring onions, shredded

For the dressing

5 tbsp peanut butter

2 tbsp sweet chilli sauce

juice of 1 lime

salt and ground black pepper

1 Put all the salad ingredients into a large salad bowl.

2 To make the dressing, put the peanut butter, chilli sauce and lime juice in a small bowl and mix together well. Season with salt and pepper. Add 2–3 tbsp cold water, a tablespoon at a time, to thin the dressing if it's too thick to pour. Use just enough water to make the dressing the right consistency.

3 Drizzle the dressing over the salad, toss together and serve.

EASY	NUTRITIONAL INFORMATION		Serves
Preparation Time 10 minutes	**Per Serving** 215 calories, 9g fat (of which 2g saturates), 9g carbohydrate, 0.6g salt	Gluten free • Dairy free	**4**

Try Something Different

Use mixed beans or flageolet beans instead of borlotti beans.

Bean and Chorizo Salad

400g can borlotti beans, drained and rinsed

4 large celery sticks, finely sliced

75g (3oz) chorizo sausage, diced

2 shallots, finely chopped

2 tbsp freshly chopped flat-leafed parsley

grated zest of ½ lemon plus 1 tbsp lemon juice

4 tbsp extra virgin olive oil

salt and ground black pepper

1 Put the borlotti beans in a large bowl and add the celery, chorizo, shallots and parsley.

2 To make the dressing, whisk together the lemon zest, lemon juice and olive oil in a small bowl. Season with salt and pepper, and whisk again to combine.

3 Pour the dressing over the bean mixture, toss together and serve.

Serves 4	EASY		NUTRITIONAL INFORMATION	
	Preparation Time 15 minutes		**Per Serving** 295 calories, 19g fat (of which 4g saturates), 20g carbohydrate, 1.9g salt	Dairy free

Get Ahead

Make the dressing (step 1), then cover and store in a screw-topped jar in the refrigerator for up to five days. **To use** Complete the recipe.

2 large Braeburn or Cox apples, about 450g (1lb), quartered, cored and sliced

450g (1lb) fennel bulb, halved, centre core removed and thinly sliced lengthways

75g (3oz) shelled pecan nuts

300g (11oz) cooked ham, cut into wide strips

1 chicory head, divided into leaves

fresh flat-leafed parsley sprigs to garnish

Apple, Chicory, Ham and Pecan Salad

For the poppy seed dressing

1 tsp runny honey

2 tsp German or Dijon mustard

3 tbsp cider vinegar

9 tbsp vegetable oil

2 tsp poppy seeds

salt and ground black pepper

1 To make the dressing, whisk together the honey, mustard and vinegar in a small bowl. Season with salt and pepper. Whisk in the oil, then the poppy seeds, and put to one side.

2 Put the ingredients for the salad in a large bowl, and toss with the dressing. Check the seasoning and adjust if necessary. Garnish with parsley sprigs and serve immediately.

EASY	**NUTRITIONAL INFORMATION**		Serves
Preparation Time 15 minutes	**Per Serving** 340 calories, 28g fat (of which 3g saturates), 10g carbohydrate, 1.6g salt	Gluten free • Dairy free	**6**

Soups and Light Meals

Cook's Tip

Miso (fermented barley and soya beans) is a living food in the same way that yogurt is and contains bacteria and enzymes that are destroyed by boiling. Miso is best added as a flavouring at the end of cooking. It's available from Asian shops and larger supermarkets.

Mushroom, Spinach and Miso Soup

1 tbsp vegetable oil

1 onion, finely sliced

125g (4oz) shiitake mushrooms, finely sliced

225g (8oz) baby spinach leaves

1.1 litres (2 pints) fresh fish stock

4 tbsp mugi miso (see Cook's Tip)

1 Heat the oil in a large pan over a low heat, add the onion and cook gently for 15 minutes until soft.

2 Add the mushrooms and cook for 5 minutes, then stir in the spinach and stock. Heat for 3 minutes, then stir in the miso – don't boil, as miso is a live culture. Spoon the soup into warmed bowls and serve hot.

Serves 6	EASY		NUTRITIONAL INFORMATION	
	Preparation Time 5 minutes	**Cooking Time** 25 minutes	**Per Serving** 55 calories, 2g fat (of which trace saturates), 6g carbohydrate, 1.3g salt	Gluten free • Dairy free

1 small baguette, thinly sliced

2 tbsp basil-infused olive oil, plus extra to drizzle

450g (1lb) frozen peas, thawed

600ml (1 pint) vegetable stock

salt and ground black pepper

Easy Pea Soup

1 Preheat the oven to 220°C (200°C fan oven) mark 7. To make the croûtons, put the bread on a baking sheet, drizzle with 2 tbsp oil and bake for 10–15 minutes until golden.

2 Meanwhile, put the peas in a food processor, add the stock and season with salt and pepper. Whiz for 2–3 minutes.

3 Pour the soup into a pan and bring to the boil, then reduce the heat and simmer for 10 minutes. Spoon into warmed bowls, add the croûtons, drizzle with extra oil and sprinkle with salt and pepper. Serve immediately.

EASY		NUTRITIONAL INFORMATION		Serves
Preparation Time 2 minutes, plus thawing	**Cooking Time** 15 minutes	**Per Serving** 408 calories, 9g fat (of which 2g saturates), 69g carbohydrate, 1.8g salt	Vegetarian • Dairy free	**4**

Fast Fish Soup

1 leek, finely chopped

4 fat garlic cloves, crushed

3 celery sticks, finely chopped

1 small fennel bulb, finely chopped

1 red chilli, seeded and finely chopped (see page 38)

3 tbsp olive oil

50ml (2fl oz) dry white wine

about 750g (1lb 11oz) mixed fish and shellfish, such as haddock and monkfish fillets, peeled and deveined raw prawns, and fresh mussels, scrubbed and cleaned (discard any mussels that don't close when tapped on a worksurface or that have broken shells)

4 tomatoes, chopped

20g (³/₄oz) fresh thyme, chopped

salt and ground black pepper

1 Put the leek into a large pan, and add the garlic, celery, fennel, chilli and olive oil. Cook over a medium heat for 5 minutes or until the vegetables are soft and beginning to colour.

2 Stir in 1.1 litres (2 pints) boiling water and the wine. Bring to the boil, then cover and simmer for 5 minutes.

3 Cut the white fish into large chunks. Add to the soup with the tomatoes and thyme. Continue to simmer gently until the fish has just turned opaque. Add the prawns, simmer for 1 minute, then add the mussels, if you're using them.

4 As soon as all the mussels have opened (discard any that do not), season the soup with salt and pepper. Ladle into four warmed bowls and serve immediately.

Try Something Different

To give the soup more of a kick, stir in 2 tbsp Pernod instead of the wine.

Garlic croûtes are traditionally served with fish soup; they can be made while the soup is simmering. Toast small slices of baguette, spread with garlic mayonnaise and sprinkle with grated cheese. Float in the hot soup just before serving.

EASY		NUTRITIONAL INFORMATION		Serves
Preparation Time 10 minutes	**Cooking Time** about 15 minutes	**Per Serving** 269 calories, 10g fat (of which 2g saturates), 6g carbohydrate, 0.4g salt	Gluten free • Dairy free	**4**

15g (½oz) dried porcini or shiitake mushrooms

2 tbsp groundnut oil

225g (8oz) fillet steak, cut into thin strips

1.1 litres (2 pints) beef stock

2 tbsp Thai fish sauce (nam pla), plus extra if needed

1 large fresh red chilli, seeded and finely chopped (see page 38)

1 lemongrass stalk, trimmed and thinly sliced

2.5cm (1in) piece of fresh root ginger, peeled and finely chopped

6 spring onions, halved lengthways and cut into 2.5cm (1in) lengths

1 garlic clove, crushed

¼ tsp caster sugar

50g (2oz) medium egg noodles

125g (4oz) fresh spinach leaves, roughly chopped

4 tbsp freshly chopped coriander

ground black pepper

Spicy Beef and Noodle Soup

1 Break the dried mushrooms into pieces, and soak in 150ml (¼ pint) boiling water for 15 minutes.

2 Meanwhile, heat the oil in a large pan over a medium heat, brown the meat in two batches and keep to one side. Pour the stock into the pan with 2 tbsp fish sauce. Add the mushrooms and their soaking liquor, the chilli, lemongrass, ginger, spring onions, garlic and sugar. Bring to the boil.

3 Break the noodles up slightly and add to the pan, then stir gently until they begin to separate. Simmer for 4–5 minutes until the noodles are just tender, stirring occasionally.

4 Stir in the spinach, coriander and reserved steak. Check and adjust the seasoning with pepper, and add a little more fish sauce if necessary. Spoon into four warmed bowls and serve hot.

	EASY		NUTRITIONAL INFORMATION	
Serves **4**	**Preparation Time** 10 minutes, plus soaking	**Cooking Time** 10 minutes	**Per Serving** 215 calories, 13g fat (of which 3g saturates), 11g carbohydrate, 1.2g salt	Dairy free

Thai Chicken Soup

1 tbsp vegetable oil

1 small onion, sliced

300g (11oz) stir-fry chicken pieces

1–2 tbsp Thai red curry paste

600ml (1 pint) hot chicken stock

400g can chopped plum tomatoes

100g (3½oz) sugarsnap peas, halved if large

150g (5oz) baby sweetcorn, halved if large

4 tbsp freshly chopped coriander

grated zest of ½ lime, plus 4 lime wedges to serve

1 Heat the oil in a large frying pan or wok over a medium heat. Add the onion and fry for 5 minutes until it begins to soften. Add the chicken and cook for a further 5 minutes until golden brown, then add the curry paste and fry for another minute to warm the spices through and release the flavours.

2 Pour in the hot chicken stock and tomatoes, then simmer for 5 minutes. Add the sugarsnap peas and sweetcorn and cook for a further minute or so until the chicken is cooked through. Divide the soup among four warmed bowls, sprinkle with the coriander and lime zest, and serve with lime wedges to squeeze over.

EASY		NUTRITIONAL INFORMATION		Serves
Preparation Time 5 minutes	**Cooking Time** 17 minutes	**Per Serving** 175 calories, 7g fat (of which 1g saturates), 7g carbohydrate, 1.2g salt	Gluten free • Dairy free	**4**

Mozzarella Mushrooms

8 large portobello mushrooms

8 slices marinated red pepper

8 fresh basil leaves

150g (5oz) mozzarella, cut into 8 slices

4 English muffins, halved

salt and ground black pepper

green salad to serve

1. Preheat the oven to 200°C (fan oven 180°C) mark 6. Lay the mushrooms side by side in a roasting tin and season with salt and pepper. Top each mushroom with a slice of red pepper and a basil leaf. Next, lay a slice of mozzarella on top of each mushroom. Season again. Roast in the oven for 15–20 minutes until the mushrooms are tender and the cheese has melted.

2. Meanwhile, toast the muffin halves until golden. Put a mozzarella mushroom on top of each muffin half. Serve immediately with a green salad.

Serves 4	EASY		NUTRITIONAL INFORMATION	
	Preparation Time 2–3 minutes	**Cooking Time** 15–20 minutes	**Per Serving** 137 calories, 8.5g fat (of which 5g saturates), 5g carbohydrate, 0.4g salt	Vegetarian

Tomato Crostini with Feta and Basil

1 small garlic clove, crushed

3 tbsp freshly chopped basil, plus extra basil leaves to garnish

25g (1oz) pinenuts

2 tbsp extra virgin olive oil

grated zest and juice of 1 lime

50g (2oz) feta cheese

4 large tomatoes, preferably vine-ripened, thickly sliced

1 x 150g tub fresh tomato salsa

50g (2oz) pitted black olives, roughly chopped

4 thick slices country-style bread

salt and ground black pepper

1 Whiz the garlic, chopped basil, pinenuts, olive oil, lime zest and juice together in a food processor to form a smooth paste. Add the feta cheese and blend until smooth. Thin with 1 tbsp water if necessary. Season with salt and pepper.

2 Put the tomatoes, salsa and olives in a bowl, and gently toss together.

3 Toast the bread. Divide the tomato mixture among the slices of toast and spoon the basil and feta mixture over the top. Garnish with basil leaves, and serve.

EASY		NUTRITIONAL INFORMATION		Serves
Preparation Time 20 minutes	**Cooking Time** 3 minutes	**Per Serving** 242 calories, 17g fat (of which 3g saturates), 18g carbohydrate, 1.5g salt	Vegetarian	**4**

Artichoke and Goat's Cheese Toasts

1 x 225g jar marinated artichokes, drained and oil reserved

225g (8oz) firm goat's cheese, rind removed and diced

1 tbsp freshly chopped thyme leaves, plus extra thyme sprigs to garnish

grated zest of 1 lemon and 1 tbsp lemon juice

1/2 tsp wholegrain mustard

4 thick slices flavoured bread, such as olive or rosemary

75g (3oz) Serrano or Parma ham slices

salt and ground black pepper

olive oil to drizzle

crushed black pepper to garnish

1 Halve the artichokes and put in a large bowl with the goat's cheese and chopped thyme.

2 Whisk together the lemon zest and juice, mustard and 3 tbsp of the reserved artichoke oil. Season with salt and pepper, whisk to combine, then stir into the artichoke mixture.

3 Toast the bread. Divide the artichoke mixture among the slices of toast and arrange the ham slices on top. Drizzle with a little olive oil, garnish with thyme sprigs and crushed black pepper and serve immediately.

Cook's Tip

Serrano ham is Spanish cured ham, made in the same way as Parma ham.

Serves 4	EASY		NUTRITIONAL INFORMATION
	Preparation Time 15 minutes	**Cooking Time** 3 minutes	**Per Serving** 371 calories, 22g fat (of which 11g saturates), 26g carbohydrate, 2.1g salt

Cook's Tip

If you want to cut down on the fat, omit the olive oil and replace the soured cream with fat-free Greek yogurt.

Tuna on Toasted Olive Bread

2 x 185g cans tuna chunks in oil, drained and oil reserved

8 spring onions, chopped

1 yellow pepper, seeded and sliced

20 kalamata olives, pitted and halved

2 tbsp extra virgin olive oil

1 tbsp white wine vinegar

1 tsp soured cream, plus extra to serve

8 thick slices olive bread

a handful of rocket

salt and ground black pepper

1 Put the tuna in a bowl with the spring onions, yellow pepper and olives.

2 In a separate bowl, whisk 2 tbsp of the reserved tuna oil with the olive oil, vinegar and soured cream. Toss into the tuna mixture.

3 Toast the bread until golden. Divide the tuna mixture among the slices of toast, then scatter over a handful of rocket. Serve immediately, with extra soured cream in a small bowl.

Serves 4	EASY		NUTRITIONAL INFORMATION
	Preparation Time 10 minutes	**Cooking Time** 3 minutes	**Per Serving** 423 calories, 18g fat (of which 6g saturates), 36g carbohydrate, 2.3g salt

Cook's Tip

Make your own spicy seasoning by mixing 1 crushed garlic clove, 1 tsp ground ginger and ¹/₂–1 tsp cayenne pepper. Toss with the pork and complete the recipe.

Pork Pittas with Salsa

1 tbsp olive oil

500g (1lb 2oz) diced pork

4 tbsp spicy seasoning such as fajita seasoning

4 large pittas

100g (3¹/₂oz) Greek yogurt

For the salsa

1 red onion, chopped

1 ripe avocado, halved, stoned, peeled and chopped

4 large tomatoes, roughly chopped

a small handful of roughly chopped fresh coriander

juice of 1 lime

salt and ground black pepper

1   Heat the oil in a pan over a medium heat and cook the pork, stirring, for 3–4 minutes. Add the spicy seasoning and stir to coat the pork, then cook for a further 4–5 minutes until cooked through.

2   Meanwhile, make the salsa. Put the onion in a bowl and add the avocado, tomatoes, coriander and lime juice. Mix well, season with salt and pepper, and put to one side.

3   Toast the pittas until lightly golden, then slit down the side and stuff with the pork, a spoonful of salsa and a dollop of Greek yogurt. Serve immediately.

EASY		NUTRITIONAL INFORMATION	Serves
Preparation Time 10 minutes	**Cooking Time** 10 minutes	**Per Serving** 518 calories, 17g fat (of which 5g saturates), 58g carbohydrate, 1.3g salt	**4**

Mushroom Soufflé Omelette

50g (2oz) small chestnut mushrooms, sliced

3 tbsp crème fraîche

2 medium eggs, separated

15g (½oz) butter

5 fresh chives, roughly chopped

salt and ground black pepper

1 Heat a non-stick frying pan for 30 seconds. Add the mushrooms and cook, stirring, for 3 minutes to brown slightly, then stir in the crème fraîche and turn off the heat.

2 Lightly beat the egg yolks in a bowl, add 2 tbsp cold water and season with salt and pepper.

3 In a separate bowl, whisk the egg whites until stiff but not dry, then gently fold into the egg yolks. Do not overmix. Heat an 18cm (7in) non-stick frying pan over a medium heat. Add the butter, then the egg mixture, tilting the pan to cover the base. Cook for 3 minutes or until the underside is golden brown.

4 Meanwhile, preheat the grill. Gently reheat the mushrooms and add the chives. Put the omelette under the grill for 1 minute or until the surface is just firm and puffy. Tip the mushroom mixture on top. Run a spatula around and underneath the omelette to loosen it, then carefully fold it and turn out onto a plate. Serve immediately.

Serves 1	EASY		NUTRITIONAL INFORMATION	
	Preparation Time 5 minutes	**Cooking Time** 7–10 minutes	**Per Serving** 440 calories, 42g fat (of which 23g saturates), 2g carbohydrate, 0.6g salt	Vegetarian Gluten free

6 tbsp olive oil

450g (1lb) potatoes, very thinly sliced

225g (8oz) onions, thinly sliced

2 garlic cloves, finely chopped

50g (2oz) sliced chorizo, cut into thin strips

6 large eggs, lightly beaten

salt and ground black pepper

Potato and Chorizo Tortilla

1 Heat the oil in an 18cm (7in) non-stick frying pan over a medium-low heat. Add the potatoes, onions and garlic. Stir together until coated in the oil, then cover the pan. Cook gently, stirring from time to time, for 10–15 minutes until the potato is soft. Season with salt, then add the chorizo.

2 Preheat the grill until hot. Season the beaten eggs with salt and pepper, and pour over the potato mixture. Cook over a medium heat for 5 minutes or until beginning to brown at the edges and the egg is about three-quarters set. Put the pan under the grill to brown the top. The egg should be a little soft in the middle, as it continues to cook and set as it cools.

3 Carefully loosen the tortilla around the edge and underneath with a flexible turner or spatula. Cut into wedges and serve.

EASY		**NUTRITIONAL INFORMATION**		**Serves**
Preparation Time 5 minutes	**Cooking Time** 25 minutes	**Per Serving** 431 calories, 32g fat (of which 7g saturates), 23g carbohydrate, 0.9g salt	Vegetarian Dairy free	**4**

Roasted Vegetable and Rocket Tartlets

375g pack ready-rolled puff pastry (preferably made with butter)

1 medium egg, beaten

2 tbsp coarse sea salt

300g (11oz) vegetable antipasti in oil (mixed roasted peppers, artichokes, onions, etc)

a little olive oil (if needed)

2 tbsp balsamic vinegar

200g (7oz) red pepper hummus

50g (2oz) wild rocket

salt and ground black pepper

1 Preheat the oven to 220°C (200°C fan oven) mark 7. Unroll the puff pastry on a lightly floured surface and cut it into six equal-sized squares.

2 Lay the pastry squares on a large baking sheet, and prick each one all over with a fork. Brush all over with the beaten egg, and sprinkle the edges of each square with sea salt. Bake in the oven for 5–7 minutes until the pastry is golden brown and cooked through.

3 Pour off 4 tbsp olive oil from the antipasti (you may need to add a little extra olive oil) into a bowl. Add the balsamic vinegar. Season well with salt and pepper, then put to one side.

4 To serve, divide the hummus among the six pastry bases, spreading it over each one. Put each pastry square on an individual plate and spoon over the vegetable antipasti – there's no need to be neat. Whisk the reserved balsamic vinegar dressing together. Add the rocket leaves and toss to coat, then pile a small handful of leaves on top of each tartlet. Serve immediately.

EASY		NUTRITIONAL INFORMATION		Serves
Preparation Time 15 minutes	**Cooking Time** 5–7 minutes	**Per Serving** 378 calories, 28g fat (of which 1g saturates), 28g carbohydrate, 1.9g salt	Vegetarian	**6**

3

Simple Suppers

Chilli Bean Cake

3 tbsp olive oil

75g (3oz) wholemeal breadcrumbs

1 bunch of spring onions, finely chopped

1 orange pepper, seeded and chopped

1 small green chilli, seeded and finely chopped (see page 38)

1 garlic clove, crushed

1 tsp ground turmeric (optional)

400g can mixed beans, drained

3 tbsp mayonnaise

a small handful of fresh basil, chopped

salt and ground black pepper

soured cream, freshly chopped coriander and lime wedges to serve (optional)

1 Heat 2 tbsp of the olive oil in a non-stick frying pan over a medium heat and fry 75g (3oz) wholemeal breadcrumbs until golden and beginning to crisp. Remove and put to one side.

2 Using the same pan, add the remaining 1 tbsp oil, and fry the spring onions until soft and golden. Add the orange pepper, chilli, garlic and turmeric, if using. Cook, stirring, for 5 minutes.

3 Tip in the beans, mayonnaise, two-thirds of the fried breadcrumbs and the basil. Season with salt and pepper, mash roughly with a fork, then press the mixture down to flatten. Sprinkle over the remaining breadcrumbs. Fry the bean cake over a medium heat for 4–5 minutes until the base is golden. Remove from the heat, cut into wedges and serve with soured cream, coriander and lime wedges if you like.

Serves 4	EASY		NUTRITIONAL INFORMATION	
	Preparation Time 10 minutes	**Cooking Time** 20 minutes	**Per Serving** 265 calories, 6g fat (of which 1g saturates), 41g carbohydrate, 2.1g salt	Vegetarian Dairy free

▽ Chickpea and Butternut Pot
▷ Cheat's Raspberry Ice Cream (see page 113)

1 large butternut squash, peeled, seeded and chopped

2 tbsp smooth peanut butter

900ml (1½ pints) hot vegetable stock

2 tbsp olive oil

2 large onions, finely chopped

1 small red chilli, seeded and finely chopped (see page 38)

2 tsp mild curry paste

225g (8oz) baby sweetcorn

2 x 400g cans chickpeas, drained and rinsed

a handful of freshly chopped coriander

salt and ground black pepper

Chickpea and Butternut Pot

1 Put the butternut squash, peanut butter and hot vegetable stock in a large pan and simmer for 10 minutes until tender. Remove three-quarters of the squash with a slotted spoon and put to one side. Mash the remaining squash into the liquid, then put the reserved squash back in the pan.

2 Meanwhile, heat the olive oil in a pan over a low heat and fry the onion, chilli, curry paste and corn until the onion is soft and caramelised, then tip the contents of the pan into the squash.

3 Add the chickpeas and coriander, and stir through. Season with salt and pepper and cook for 4–5 minutes until piping hot. Serve immediately.

EASY		NUTRITIONAL INFORMATION		Serves
Preparation Time 10 minutes	**Cooking Time** 15–20 minutes	**Per Serving** 307 calories, 14g fat (of which 2g saturates), 34g carbohydrate, 2.8g salt	Vegetarian Gluten free • Dairy free	**4**

Try Something Different

Try marinated peppers, artichokes or chargrilled aubergines instead of the olives and sunblush tomatoes.

6 tbsp tomato pizza sauce

2 pizzeria-style pizza bases

100g (3¹/₂oz) soft goat's cheese

1 red onion, finely sliced

100g (3¹/₂oz) sunblush tomatoes

100g (3¹/₂oz) olives

a handful of fresh basil, roughly torn

green salad to serve

Deli Pizza

1 Put a large baking sheet on the top shelf of the oven, and preheat the oven to 220°C (200°C fan oven) mark 7.

2 Spread a thin layer of the tomato sauce over each of the pizza bases, leaving a 2.5cm (1in) border round the edge. Top with dollops of goat's cheese, then scatter over the red onion, tomatoes and olives.

3 Slide one of the pizzas on to the hot baking sheet and bake for 15 minutes or until golden and crisp. Repeat with the second pizza base. Scatter over the torn basil, and serve immediately with a green salad.

	EASY		NUTRITIONAL INFORMATION	
Serves	**Preparation Time**	**Cooking Time**	**Per Serving**	
4	5 minutes	15 minutes	440 calories, 15g fat (of which 5g saturates), 64g carbohydrate, 2.8g salt	Vegetarian

Cook's Tip

Make Parmesan shavings with a vegetable peeler. Hold the piece of cheese in one hand, and pare off wafer-thin strips of cheese using the peeler.

Fusilli with Chilli and Tomatoes

350g (12oz) fusilli or other short dried pasta

4 tbsp olive oil

1 large red chilli, seeded and finely chopped (see page 38)

1 garlic clove, crushed

500g (1lb 2oz) cherry tomatoes

2 tbsp freshly chopped basil

50g (2oz) Parmesan, shaved (see Cook's Tip)

salt and ground black pepper

1 Cook the pasta in a large pan of lightly salted boiling water according to the packet instructions. Drain.

2 Meanwhile, heat the oil in a large frying pan over a high heat. Add the chilli and garlic, and cook for 30 seconds. Add the tomato, season with salt and pepper, and cook over a high heat for 3 minutes or until the skins begin to split.

3 Add the basil and drained pasta, and toss together. Transfer to a serving dish, sprinkle the Parmesan shavings over the top and serve immediately.

EASY		NUTRITIONAL INFORMATION		Serves
Preparation Time 10 minutes	**Cooking Time** 10–15 minutes	**Per Serving** 479 calories, 17g fat (of which 4g saturates), 69g carbohydrate, 0.4g salt	Vegetarian	**4**

Ribbon Pasta with Courgettes and Capers

450g (1lb) dried pappardelle pasta

2 large courgettes, coarsely grated

50g can anchovies in oil, drained and roughly chopped

1 red chilli, seeded and finely chopped (see page 38)

2 tbsp salted capers, rinsed

1 garlic clove, crushed

4 tbsp pitted black kalamata olives, roughly chopped

4 tbsp extra virgin olive oil

2 tbsp freshly chopped flat-leafed parsley

1 To save time, prepare the other ingredients while the pasta is cooking. Cook the pappardelle in a large pan of lightly salted boiling water according to the packet instructions. About 1 minute before the end of the cooking time, add the courgette, then simmer until the pasta is al dente.

2 Meanwhile, put the anchovies into a small pan over a low heat. Add the chilli, capers, garlic, olives and olive oil and cook, stirring, for 2–3 minutes.

3 Drain the pasta and put back in the pan. Pour the hot anchovy mixture on top, mix well and toss through the parsley. Season with salt and pepper, and serve immediately.

Cook's Tip

For a vegetarian alternative, omit the anchovies and serve with freshly grated vegetarian Parmesan instead.

EASY

Preparation Time	Cooking Time
5 minutes	10–15 minutes

NUTRITIONAL INFORMATION

Per Serving
544 calories, 16g fat (of which 2g saturates),
85g carbohydrate, 2.1g salt

Dairy free

Serves
4

Penne with Smoked Salmon

350g (12oz) penne or other short tubular dried pasta

200ml (7fl oz) half-fat crème fraîche

150g (5oz) smoked salmon, roughly chopped

20g (³/₄oz) fresh dill, finely chopped

salt and ground black pepper

lemon wedges to serve (optional)

1 Cook the pasta in a large pan of lightly salted boiling water according to the packet instructions. Drain.

2 Meanwhile, put the crème fraîche in a large bowl. Add the smoked salmon and dill, season well with salt and pepper, and mix together. Gently stir through the drained penne, and serve immediately with lemon wedges, if you like, to squeeze over.

Serves 4	EASY		NUTRITIONAL INFORMATION
	Preparation Time 5 minutes	**Cooking Time** 10–15 minutes	**Per Serving** 432 calories, 11g fat (of which 6g saturates), 67g carbohydrate, 1.7g salt

▼ Pesto Cod with Butter Beans
▶ Rich Chocolate Pots (see page 125)

Pesto Cod with Butter Beans

4 small cod fillets

4 tbsp red pepper pesto

a generous glug of olive oil

2 x 400g cans butter beans, drained

2 garlic cloves, crushed

225g (8oz) fresh spinach

a squeeze of lemon juice

1 Preheat the grill to medium. Spread each cod fillet evenly with a tablespoon of the red pesto, and grill for 10–15 minutes until the flesh is opaque and just cooked.

2 Meanwhile, heat the oil in a pan and add the butter beans and garlic. Cook for 10 minutes, stirring occasionally and mashing the beans lightly as you do so.

3 Two or three minutes before serving, add the spinach to the pan and allow it to wilt. Spoon the butter beans on to four warmed plates, and top with the cod and any juices from grilling. Squeeze a little lemon juice over each piece of fish, and serve immediately.

EASY		NUTRITIONAL INFORMATION		Serves
Preparation Time 5 minutes	**Cooking Time** 15 minutes	**Per Serving** 403 calories, 16g fat (of which 3g saturates), 24g carbohydrate, 2.5g salt	Gluten free	**4**

Prawn and Peanut Noodles

300g (11oz) straight-to-wok noodles

360g pack stir-fry vegetables

4 tbsp coconut cream

4 tbsp smooth peanut butter

1 tbsp Thai red or green curry paste

juice of ½ lime

225g (8oz) cooked peeled king prawns

a small handful of freshly chopped coriander

25g (1oz) peanuts, chopped

▲ Prawn and Peanut Noodles
▶ Marinated Strawberries (see page 123)

1 Put the noodles and stir-fry vegetables into a large bowl or wok and cover with boiling water. Cover with clingfilm and leave for 5 minutes.

2 Meanwhile, mix together the coconut cream, peanut butter, curry paste and lime juice in a bowl.

3 Drain the noodles and vegetables in a colander. Put back in the bowl and toss with the prawns, coriander and half the dressing. Sprinkle with the peanuts and serve with the remaining dressing.

Cook's Tip

Ready-prepared stir-fry vegetables make this extra-quick, but if you can't find them, try a mixture of three or four of the following: strips of red, orange or yellow peppers, baby sweetcorn, mangetouts or sugarsnaps, carrots cut into matchsticks, bean sprouts.

Serves 4	EASY	NUTRITIONAL INFORMATION	
	Preparation Time 10 minutes, plus 5 minutes soaking	**Per Serving** 579 calories, 24g fat (of which 7g saturates), 67g carbohydrate, 0.7g salt	Dairy free

Cook's Tips

If the mackerel are large, make three shallow slashes on either side of the fish.

To test whether the fish is cooked, prise the flesh from the backbone with a knife; it should be opaque and come away easily.

Peppered Mackerel

4 tsp whole mixed peppercorns

4 fresh mackerel, gutted, about 250g (9oz) each

1 tbsp sunflower oil

200ml (7fl oz) crème fraîche

lemon wedges to garnish

asparagus and sugarsnap peas to serve

1 Lightly crush 2 tsp of the peppercorns using a mortar and pestle. Sprinkle one side of each mackerel with half the crushed peppercorns.

2 Heat the oil in a frying pan over a medium-high heat. Add the fish, peppered side down, and cook for 5–7 minutes. Sprinkle the mackerel with the remaining crushed peppercorns, turn the fish over and continue to fry for 5–7 minutes until cooked (see Cook's Tips). Remove and keep warm.

3 Wipe out the pan, add the crème fraîche and bring to the boil. Stir in the remaining whole peppercorns. (If the sauce becomes too thick, add some boiling water.)

4 To serve, spoon the sauce over the mackerel, garnish with lemon wedges and serve with asparagus and sugarsnap peas.

Serves 4	EASY		NUTRITIONAL INFORMATION	
	Preparation Time 10 minutes	**Cooking Time** 15 minutes	**Per Serving** 764 calories, 63g fat (of which 22g saturates), 1g carbohydrate, 0.4g salt	Gluten free

Cook's Tip

Smoked fish is quite salty, so always taste the sauce before seasoning with any extra salt.

Simple Smoked Haddock

25g (1oz) unsalted butter

1 tbsp olive oil

1 garlic clove, thinly sliced

4 thick smoked haddock or cod fillets, about 175g (6oz) each

a small handful of freshly chopped parsley (optional)

finely grated zest of 1 small lemon, plus lemon wedges to serve

romanesco, cauliflower or broccoli to serve

1 Heat the butter, oil and garlic in a large non-stick pan over a high heat until the mixture starts to foam and sizzle. Put the fish into the pan, skin side down, and fry for 10 minutes – this will give a golden crust underneath the fish.

2 Carefully turn the fish over. Scatter the parsley, if using, and lemon zest over each fillet, then fry for a further 30 seconds. Put a cooked fillet on each of four warmed plates, and spoon over some of the buttery juices. Serve with the lemon wedges and steamed romanesco, cauliflower or broccoli.

EASY		NUTRITIONAL INFORMATION		Serves
Preparation Time 10 minutes	**Cooking Time** about 10 minutes	**Per Serving** 217 calories, 9g fat (of which 4g saturates), 1g carbohydrate, 3.4g salt	Gluten free	**4**

▽ Chicken with Wine and Capers

▷ Quick Lemon Mousse (see page 115)

Chicken with Wine and Capers

1 tbsp olive oil

15g (½ oz) butter

4 small skinless chicken breasts

lemon wedges to garnish

boiled rice to serve

For the wine and caper sauce

125ml (4fl oz) white wine

3 tbsp capers, rinsed and drained

juice of 1 lemon

15g (½oz) butter

1 tbsp freshly chopped flat-leafed parsley

1 Heat the oil and butter in a frying pan over a medium heat. Add the chicken breasts and fry over a medium heat for 10–12 minutes on each side until cooked through. Transfer to a warm plate, cover and keep warm.

2 To make the sauce, add the wine and capers to the same pan. Bring to the boil, then simmer for 2–3 minutes until the wine is reduced by half. Add the lemon juice and butter, and stir in the parsley.

3 Divide the chicken among four warmed plates, pour the sauce over the chicken, garnish each serving with a lemon wedge and serve immediately with boiled rice.

Serves	EASY		NUTRITIONAL INFORMATION	
4	**Preparation Time** 5 minutes	**Cooking Time** 25 minutes	**Per Serving** 234 calories, 10g fat (of which 5g saturates), trace carbohydrate, 0.3g salt	Gluten free

Try Something Different

Instead of lemons, use limes. Knead them on the worktop for 30 seconds before squeezing so they give as much juice as possible.

4 small chicken breasts, cut into chunky strips

juice of 2 lemons

2 tbsp olive oil

4–6 tbsp demerara sugar

salt

green salad to serve

Lemon Chicken

1 Put the chicken in a large bowl, and season with salt. Add the lemon juice and olive oil and stir to mix.

2 Preheat the grill to medium. Spread the chicken out on a large flat baking sheet, and sprinkle over half the sugar. Grill for 3–4 minutes until caramelised, then turn the chicken over, sprinkle with the remaining sugar and grill until the chicken is cooked through and golden.

3 Divide the chicken among four plates, and serve with a green salad.

EASY		NUTRITIONAL INFORMATION		Serves
Preparation Time 2 minutes	**Cooking Time** 6–8 minutes	**Per Serving** 231 calories, 7g fat (of which 1g saturates), 13g carbohydrate. 0.2g salt	Gluten free	**4**

Basil and Lemon Chicken

grated zest of 1 lemon, plus 4 tbsp lemon juice

1 tsp caster sugar

1 tsp Dijon mustard

175ml (6fl oz) lemon-infused oil

4 tbsp freshly chopped basil

2 x 210g packs roast chicken

250g (9oz) baby leaf spinach

55g pack crisp bacon, broken into small pieces

salt and ground black pepper

▷ **Easy Pea Soup (see page 51)**

▲ **Basil and Lemon Chicken**

▷ **Amaretti with Lemon Mascarpone (see page 126)**

1 Put the lemon zest and juice, sugar, mustard and oil in a small bowl. Season with salt and pepper. Whisk together until thoroughly combined, then add the basil.

2 Remove any bones from the roast chicken, leave the skin attached and slice into five or six pieces. Arrange the sliced chicken in a dish and pour the dressing over, then cover and leave to marinate for at least 15 minutes.

3 Just before serving, lift the chicken from the dressing and put to one side.

4 Put the spinach in a large bowl, pour the dressing over and toss together. Arrange the chicken on top of the spinach, and sprinkle with the bacon. Serve immediately.

EASY

Preparation Time
15 minutes, plus minimum 15 minutes marinating

NUTRITIONAL INFORMATION

Per Serving
331 calories, 25g fat (of which 5g saturates),
2g carbohydrate, 1.3g salt

Gluten free • Dairy free

Serves
4

700g (1½lb) new potatoes, scrubbed, halved if large

175g (6oz) runner beans, sliced

a little sunflower or olive oil

4 pork escalopes

150ml (¼ pint) hot chicken stock

150ml (¼ pint) apple cider

2 tbsp wholegrain mustard

150g (5oz) Greek yogurt

4 fresh tarragon stems, leaves only

a squeeze of lemon juice

Flash-in-the-pan Pork

1 Cook the new potatoes in a large pan of boiling salted water for 10 minutes. Add the beans and cook for a further 5 minutes or until tender. Drain.

2 Meanwhile, heat the oil in a large non-stick frying pan over a medium heat, and cook the pork for 3 minutes on each side until browned. Remove from the pan and keep warm. Add the stock, cider and mustard to the pan, and increase the heat to reduce the liquid by half.

3 Just before serving, reduce the heat and add the yogurt, tarragon leaves and lemon juice. Put the pork back in the pan to coat with the sauce and warm through. Serve with the potatoes and beans.

Serves 4	EASY		NUTRITIONAL INFORMATION	
	Preparation Time 5 minutes	Cooking Time 15 minutes	Per Serving 346 calories, 12g fat (of which 4g saturates), 32g carbohydrate, 0.6g salt	Gluten free

Try Something Different

Instead of the papaya, use ripe mango.

Cumin-spiced Gammon

2 tbsp olive oil

large pinch of ground cumin

large pinch of paprika

2 tsp light muscovado sugar

8 thin smoked gammon steaks, each around 125g (4oz)

2 large ripe papayas

grated zest and juice of 2 limes

½ red chilli, seeded and finely chopped (see page 38)

20g (¾oz) fresh mint, finely chopped

green beans to serve

1 Preheat the grill to medium. In a small bowl, mix together the oil, cumin, paprika and half the sugar.

2 Put the gammon on a non-stick baking sheet, then brush the spiced oil over both sides. Grill the gammon for about 5 minutes on each side, basting once or twice with the juices.

3 Meanwhile, cut each papaya in half, then deseed and peel. Roughly chop half the flesh and put into a bowl. Purée the remaining fruit with the lime juice. Add to the bowl with the lime zest, chilli, mint and remaining sugar.

4 Divide the gammon among four plates, spoon the papaya mixture over the top of the gammon and serve with green beans.

EASY		**NUTRITIONAL INFORMATION**		Serves
Preparation Time 5 minutes	**Cooking Time** about 10 minutes	**Per Serving** 522 calories, 26g fat (of which 8g saturates), 18g carbohydrate, 9.7g salt	Gluten free • Dairy free	**4**

Speedy Beef Noodles

250g (9oz) fine egg noodles
4 tbsp sesame oil, plus a little extra to brush
300g (11oz) beef fillet
4 tbsp chilli soy sauce
juice of 1 lime
2 red peppers, halved, seeded and cut into thin strips
200g (7oz) mangetouts, sliced
4 tbsp freshly chopped coriander

1 Put the noodles in a large bowl and cover with boiling water. Leave to soak for 4 minutes, then rinse under cold running water and set aside.

2 Meanwhile, brush a large frying or griddle pan with a little sesame oil and heat until hot. Fry the beef for 3–4 minutes on each side (4–5 minutes if you like it well done). Remove from the pan and keep warm.

3 Add the 4 tbsp sesame oil to the pan with the chilli soy sauce, lime juice, red pepper, mangetouts and coriander, and stir to mix. Add the noodles and use two large spoons to toss them over the heat to combine with the sauce and warm through.

4 Cut the beef into thin slices and serve on a bed of noodles.

Serves	EASY		NUTRITIONAL INFORMATION	
4	**Preparation Time** 5 minutes	**Cooking Time** 10 minutes	**Per Serving** 510 calories, 19g fat (of which 5g saturates), 60g carbohydrate, 2.8g salt	Dairy free

Chilli Steak and Corn on the Cob

50g (2oz) butter, softened

1 large red chilli, seeded and finely chopped (see page 38)

1 garlic clove, crushed

25g (1oz) freshly grated Parmesan

1 tbsp finely chopped fresh basil

4 corn on the cob, each cut into three

1 tbsp olive oil

4 sirloin steaks, about 150g (5oz) each

1 Put the butter in a bowl and beat with a wooden spoon. Add the chilli, garlic, Parmesan and basil, and mix everything together. Cover and chill to firm up.

2 Meanwhile, bring a large pan of water to the boil. Add the corn, cover to bring back to the boil, then simmer, half-covered, for about 10 minutes until tender. Drain well.

3 Heat the oil in a large frying pan or griddle over a medium heat. Cook the steaks for 3–4 minutes on each side for medium-rare (4–5 minutes for medium).

4 Divide the corn and steaks among four warm plates and top with the chilled butter. Serve immediately, with a mixed green salad.

EASY		NUTRITIONAL INFORMATION		Serves
Preparation Time 5 minutes	**Cooking Time** 15 minutes	**Per Serving** 564 calories, 31g fat (of which 14g saturates), 33g carbohydrate, 1.4g salt	Gluten free	**4**

Hearty Warmers

Spiced Bean and Vegetable Stew

3 tbsp olive oil

2 small onions, sliced

2 garlic cloves, crushed

1 tbsp sweet paprika

1 small dried red chilli, seeded and finely chopped

700g (1½lb) sweet potatoes, peeled and cubed

700g (1½lb) pumpkin, peeled and cut into chunks

125g (4oz) okra, trimmed

500g (1lb 2oz) passata

400g can haricot or cannellini beans, drained and rinsed

salt and ground black pepper

1 Heat the oil in a large heavy pan over a very gentle heat. Add the onion and garlic, and cook for 5 minutes. Stir in the paprika and chilli, and cook for a further 2 minutes.

2 Add the sweet potato, pumpkin, okra, passata and 900ml (1½ pints) water. Season generously with salt and pepper. Cover, bring to the boil and simmer for 20 minutes until the vegetables are tender. Add the haricot or cannellini beans, and cook for 3 minutes to warm through. Serve immediately.

Serves 6	EASY		NUTRITIONAL INFORMATION	
	Preparation Time 5 minutes	**Cooking Time** about 30 minutes	**Per Serving** 262 calories, 7g fat (of which 1g saturates), 44g carbohydrate, 1.3g salt	Vegetarian Gluten free • Dairy free

Roast Tomato Pasta

400g (14oz) dried rigatoni pasta

700g (1½lb) cherry tomatoes

olive oil to drizzle

50g (2oz) pinenuts

a large handful of fresh basil leaves, torn

salt and ground black pepper

freshly grated Parmesan to serve

1 Preheat the oven to 240°C (220°C fan oven) mark 9. Bring a large pan of lightly salted water to the boil. Add the pasta, cover and bring back to the boil. Remove the lid and cook the pasta according to the packet instructions.

2 Meanwhile, cut half the tomatoes in two and arrange them in a large roasting tin, cut side up. Add the remaining whole tomatoes and drizzle all with olive oil. Season with salt and pepper. Put the pinenuts on to a separate roasting tray, and roast both in the oven for 15 minutes until the tomatoes are softened and lightly caramelised. Watch carefully to make sure the pinenuts don't scorch, and remove from the oven earlier if necessary.

3 Drain the pasta well and add to the roasting tin when the tomatoes are done. Scatter over the basil and pinenuts, then stir thoroughly to coat the pasta in the juices. Adjust the seasoning, and stir in a little more olive oil if you like. Sprinkle with Parmesan.

EASY		**NUTRITIONAL INFORMATION**	Serves
Preparation Time 5 minutes	**Cooking Time** 15 minutes	**Per Serving** 507 calories, 16g fat (of which 2g saturates), 80g carbohydrate, 0g salt	Vegetarian	**4**

Pesto Gnocchi

800g (1lb 12oz) fresh gnocchi
200g (7oz) green beans, trimmed and chopped
125g (4oz) fresh green pesto
10 sunblush tomatoes, roughly chopped

1 Cook the gnocchi in a large pan of lightly salted boiling water according to the packet instructions. Add the beans to the water for the last 3 minutes of cooking time.

2 Drain the gnocchi and beans and put back in the pan. Add the pesto and tomatoes and toss well. Serve immediately.

EASY		NUTRITIONAL INFORMATION		Serves
Preparation Time 10 minutes	**Cooking Time** 10 minutes	**Per Serving** 481 calories, 24g fat (of which 6g saturates), 56g carbohydrate, 0.4g salt	Vegetarian	**4**

Cook's Tip

Choose bags or bunches of fresh basil, as the larger leaves have a stronger, more peppery flavour than those of plants sold in pots.

Aubergine Parmigiana

2 large aubergines, thinly sliced lengthways

2 tbsp olive oil, plus extra to brush

3 fat garlic cloves, sliced

2 x 200ml tubs fresh napoletana sauce

4 ready-roasted red peppers, roughly chopped

20g (¾oz) fresh basil, roughly chopped (see Cook's Tip)

150g (5oz) Taleggio or fontina cheese, coarsely grated

50g (2oz) Parmesan, coarsely grated

salt and ground black pepper

1 Preheat the oven to 200°C (180°C fan oven) mark 6, and preheat the grill until hot. Put the aubergine on an oiled baking sheet, brush the aubergine with olive oil, scatter over the garlic and season with salt and pepper. Grill for 5–6 minutes until golden.

2 Spread a little napoletana sauce over the bottom of an oiled ovenproof dish, then cover with a layer of aubergine and peppers, packing the layers together as tightly as you can. Sprinkle a little basil and some of each cheese over the top. Repeat the layers, finishing with a layer of cheese. Season with pepper. Cook in the oven for 20 minutes or until golden. Serve hot.

Serves 4	EASY		NUTRITIONAL INFORMATION	
	Preparation Time 5 minutes	**Cooking Time** about 25 minutes	**Per Serving** 370 calories, 25g fat (of which 11g saturates), 17g carbohydrate, 2.1g salt	Vegetarian Gluten free

Black-Eye Bean Chilli

1 tbsp olive oil

1 onion, chopped

3 celery sticks, finely chopped

2 x 400g cans black-eye beans, drained and rinsed

2 x 400g cans chopped tomatoes

2 or 3 splashes of Tabasco sauce

3 tbsp freshly chopped coriander

4 warmed tortillas and soured cream to serve

1 Heat the oil in a frying pan. Add the onion and celery and cook for 10 minutes until softened.

2 Add the beans, tomatoes and Tabasco to the pan. Bring to the boil, then simmer for 10 minutes.

3 Just before serving, stir in the coriander. Spoon the chilli on to the warm tortillas, roll up and serve with soured cream.

EASY		NUTRITIONAL INFORMATION		Serves
Preparation Time 10 minutes	**Cooking Time** 20 minutes	**Per Serving** 245 calories, 5g fat (of which 1g saturates), 39g carbohydrate, 1.8g salt	Vegetarian	**4**

Kerala Fish Curry

4 skinless sole or plaice fillets, about 125g (4oz) each

2 tbsp light olive oil

1 onion, thinly sliced

1 large garlic clove, crushed

1 green chilli, slit lengthways, seeds in (see page 38)

2.5cm (1in) piece of fresh root ginger, grated

1 tsp ground turmeric

1 tbsp garam masala or about 12 curry leaves (see Cook's Tip)

200ml (7fl oz) coconut milk

1 tbsp freshly squeezed lime juice, white wine vinegar or tamarind paste

salt and ground black pepper

fresh banana leaves to serve (optional, see Cook's Tip)

basmati rice to serve

1 lime, cut into wedges, to serve

1 Roll up the fish fillets from head to tail, and put to one side.

2 Heat the oil in a deep frying pan over a medium heat, and stir in the onion, garlic, chilli and ginger. Keep stirring for 5–7 minutes until the onion is soft. Add the turmeric and garam masala (or curry leaves, if using) and fry for a further 1–2 minutes until aromatic.

3 Pour the coconut milk into the pan along with 200ml (7fl oz) water and bring to the boil. Reduce the heat and simmer very gently, uncovered, for 7–10 minutes until slightly thickened. The sauce should be the consistency of single cream. Stir in the lime juice, vinegar or tamarind. Check the seasoning and adjust if necessary.

4 When you're ready to serve, lower the rolls of fish into the hot sauce gently to avoid splashing, and simmer very gently for 1–2 minutes until just cooked. Serve on a bed of basmati rice, in deep bowls lined with strips of banana leaves if you like, with a wedge of lime to squeeze over.

Get Ahead

Make the sauce up to 4 hours ahead.
To use gently reheat to simmering point before you add the fish.

Cook's Tip

Buy curry leaves and banana leaves from Asian shops.

Serves 4	A LITTLE EFFORT		NUTRITIONAL INFORMATION	
	Preparation Time 10 minutes	**Cooking Time** about 20 minutes	**Per Serving** 189 calories, 9g fat (of which 1g saturates), 5g carbohydrate, 0.5g salt	Gluten free • Dairy free

Cook's Tips

Don't overcook this dish or the noodles will be soggy and the prawns tough.

Bird's-eye chillies are very hot; the smaller they are, the hotter.

Thai Noodles with Prawns

4–6 tsp Thai red curry paste

175g (6oz) medium egg noodles (wholewheat if possible)

2 small red onions, chopped

1 lemongrass stalk, trimmed and sliced

1 fresh red bird's-eye chilli, seeded and finely chopped (see Cook's Tips and page 38)

300ml (10fl oz) low-fat coconut milk

400g (14oz) raw tiger prawns, peeled

4 tbsp freshly chopped coriander, plus extra freshly torn coriander to garnish

salt and ground black pepper

1 Put 2 litres (3½ pints) boiling water in a large pan. Add the curry paste, noodles, onions, lemongrass, chilli and coconut milk. Bring to the boil, then add the prawns and the chopped coriander. Simmer for 2–3 minutes until the prawns turn pink. Season with salt and pepper.

2 To serve, divide the noodles among four large bowls, and sprinkle with the torn coriander.

Serves 4	EASY		NUTRITIONAL INFORMATION	
	Preparation Time 10 minutes	**Cooking Time** 5 minutes	**Per Serving** 343 calories, 11g fat (of which 2g saturates), 40g carbohydrate, 1g salt	Dairy free

Quick Fish and Chips

4 litres (7 pints) sunflower oil for deep-frying

125g (4oz) self-raising flour

¼ tsp baking powder

¼ tsp salt

1 medium egg

150ml (¼ pint) sparkling mineral water

2 haddock or hake fillets, about 125g (4oz) each

450g (1lb) Desirée potatoes, cut into 1cm (½in) chips

salt, vinegar and garlic mayonnaise to serve

1 Heat the oil in a deep-fryer to 190°C (test by frying a small cube of bread; it should brown in 20 seconds).

2 Whiz the flour, baking powder, salt, egg and water in a food processor until combined into a batter. (Or put the ingredients in a bowl and beat everything together until smooth.) Remove the blade and drop one of the fish fillets into the batter to coat it.

3 Put half the chips in the deep-fryer, then add the battered fish. Fry for 6 minutes until just cooked, then remove and drain well on kitchen paper. Keep warm if not serving immediately.

4 Drop the remaining fillet into the batter to coat, then repeat step 3 with the remaining chips. Serve both portions with salt, vinegar and garlic mayonnaise.

EASY		NUTRITIONAL INFORMATION		Serves
Preparation Time 15 minutes	**Cooking Time** 12 minutes	**Per Serving** 1186 calories, 79g fat (of which 18g saturates), 73g carbohydrate, 3.2g salt	Dairy free	**2**

Chicken Fajitas

4 skinless chicken breasts, about 700g (1½lb) total weight, cut into chunky strips

2 tbsp fajita seasoning (ready-made or see Cook's Tip, page 61)

1 tbsp sunflower oil

1 red pepper, seeded and sliced

360g jar fajita sauce

1 bunch of spring onions, trimmed and halved

8 large flour tortillas

150g (5oz) tomato salsa

125g (4oz) guacamole dip

150ml (¼ pint) soured cream

▲ **Chicken Fajitas**
▶ **Sticky Maple Syrup Pineapple (see page 118)**

1 Put the chicken breasts in a shallow dish and toss together with the fajita seasoning. Heat the oil in a large non-stick frying pan, add the chicken and cook for 5 minutes or until golden brown and tender.

2 Add the red pepper and cook for 2 minutes. Pour in the fajita sauce, bring to the boil and simmer for 5 minutes or until thoroughly heated. Add a splash of boiling water if the sauce becomes too thick. Stir in the spring onions and cook for 2 minutes.

3 Meanwhile, warm the tortillas in a microwave on full power for 45 seconds, or wrap in foil and warm in a preheated oven at 180°C (160°C fan oven) mark 4 for 10 minutes.

4 Transfer the chicken to a serving dish and take to the table, along with the tortillas, salsa, guacamole and soured cream. Let everyone help themselves.

EASY

Preparation Time	Cooking Time
10 minutes	10 minutes

NUTRITIONAL INFORMATION

Per Serving
651 calories, 23g fat (of which 8g saturates),
63g carbohydrate, 1.6g salt

Serves

4

Italian Sausage Stew

25g (1oz) dried porcini mushrooms

2 tbsp olive oil

1 onion, sliced

2 garlic cloves, chopped

1 small red chilli, seeded and finely chopped (see page 38)

2 fresh rosemary stalks, leaves picked

300g (11oz) whole rustic Italian salami sausages, such as salami Milano, cut into 1cm (½in) slices

400g can chopped tomatoes

200ml (7fl oz) red wine

1 tsp salt

175g (6oz) quick-cook or instant polenta

50g (2oz) butter

50g (2oz) freshly grated Parmesan, plus extra shavings to serve (optional)

75g (3oz) Fontina cheese, cubed

ground black pepper

green or mixed salad to serve

▲ Italian Sausage Stew
▶ Zabaglione (see page 122)

1 Put the mushrooms in a small bowl, pour over 100ml (3½fl oz) boiling water and leave to soak for 20 minutes, or soften in the microwave on full power for 3½ minutes. Set aside to cool.

2 Heat the oil in a large frying pan over a low heat, add the onion, garlic and chilli and cook gently for 5 minutes. Add half of the rosemary leaves to the pan, stirring.

3 Add the salami and fry for 2 minutes on each side or until browned. Drain and chop the soaked mushrooms and add to the pan. Add the tomatoes and wine, then season with pepper. Simmer, uncovered, for 5 minutes.

4 Put 750ml (1¼ pints) boiling water and the salt in a pan. Bring back to the boil, add the polenta and cook according to the packet instructions. Add the butter and both cheeses, and mix together well.

5 To serve, divide the polenta among four serving plates, and top with the Parmesan shavings, if you like. Spoon some sausage stew alongside each serving of polenta and garnish with the remaining rosemary. Serve immediately with a green or mixed side salad.

Serves	EASY		NUTRITIONAL INFORMATION
4	**Preparation Time** 10 minutes, plus soaking	**Cooking Time** 15 minutes	**Per Serving** 443 calories, 35g fat (of which 12g saturates), 6g carbohydrate, 3.4g salt

Pork with Artichokes and Beans

2 tbsp vegetable oil

2 pork fillets, about 275g (10oz) each, cut into 1cm (½in) slices

2 tbsp freshly chopped thyme leaves

8 tbsp olive oil

400g can artichoke hearts, drained, rinsed and quartered

400g can flageolet beans, drained and rinsed

185g jar pitted green olives, drained and rinsed

juice of 1 lemon

salt and ground black pepper

1 Heat the vegetable oil in a frying pan over a medium heat and fry the pork for 2 minutes on each side. Add the thyme and season with salt and pepper.

2 Meanwhile, heat the olive oil in a separate pan over a medium heat. Add the artichokes and beans, and cook for 3–4 minutes. Add the olives and lemon juice, and season with pepper.

3 Put the pork on top of the artichokes, beans and olives, and serve immediately.

Serves 4	EASY		NUTRITIONAL INFORMATION	
	Preparation Time 10 minutes	**Cooking Time** 8 minutes	**Per Serving** 473 calories, 36g fat (of which 6g saturates), 17g carbohydrate, 3.7g salt	Gluten free • Dairy free

Chicken with Black-Eye Beans and Greens

2 tsp Jamaican jerk seasoning

4 chicken breasts

1kg (2¼lb) spring greens or cabbage, core removed and shredded

2 x 300g cans black-eye beans, drained and rinsed

8 tbsp olive oil

juice of 1¼ lemons

salt and ground black pepper

1 Preheat the grill. Rub the jerk seasoning into the chicken breasts, and sprinkle with salt. Cook under the grill for 15 minutes or until done, turning from time to time.

2 Cook the spring greens or cabbage in salted boiling water until just tender – bringing the water back to the boil after adding the greens is usually enough to cook them. Drain and put back in the pan.

3 Add the beans and olive oil to the greens, and season well with salt and pepper. Heat through and add the juice of 1 lemon.

4 To serve, slice the chicken and place on the bean mixture, then drizzle over the remaining lemon juice and serve.

EASY

Preparation Time	Cooking Time
5 minutes	15 minutes

NUTRITIONAL INFORMATION

Per Serving
491 calories, 26g fat (of which 4g saturates),
31g carbohydrate, 1.5g salt

Gluten free • Dairy free

Serves
4

Lamb with Spicy Couscous

2 lamb fillets, each weighing about 400g (14oz)

5 tbsp olive oil

1 aubergine, cut into 1cm (½in) dice

1 tsp ground cumin

½ tsp ground cinnamon

225g (8oz) quick-cook couscous

1 large fresh red chilli, seeded and finely chopped (see page 38)

3 tbsp freshly chopped mint

75g (3oz) raisins, soaked in hot water and drained

salt and ground black pepper

Greek yogurt to serve

1 Trim the lamb fillets, rub in 1 tbsp of the oil and season well with salt and pepper. Heat a heavy-based non-stick pan, add the lamb and fry for 15 minutes, turning regularly. Remove from the pan and leave to rest for 5 minutes (see Cook's Tip).

2 Meanwhile, toss the aubergine in the cumin and cinnamon, and fry in 2 tbsp of the oil for 10 minutes or until softened. Prepare the couscous according to the packet instructions, then fluff the grains using a fork. Add the aubergine, chilli, 2 tbsp of the mint, the raisins and the remaining oil to the couscous. Season well with salt and pepper.

3 To serve, slice the lamb and place on the couscous. Drizzle with yogurt, sprinkle with the remaining chopped mint, and serve immediately.

Cook's Tip

Leaving the lamb to rest for 5 minutes allows the juices to set so that they don't run out.

EASY		NUTRITIONAL INFORMATION	Serves
Preparation Time 10 minutes	**Cooking Time** 15 minutes	**Per Serving** 675 calories, 37g fat (of which 13g saturates), 44g carbohydrate, 0.5g salt	**4**

Lamb with Butter Beans and Spinach

1 tbsp olive oil, plus extra to brush
1 onion, finely sliced
1 garlic clove, crushed
2 x 400g cans butter beans, drained and rinsed
200g (7oz) fresh spinach
4 small lamb chops
lemon wedges to serve

For the dressing
1 tbsp olive oil
3 tbsp low-fat yogurt
2 tbsp tahini
1 tsp harissa paste
juice of ½ lemon
salt and ground black pepper

1 Heat the oil in a large pan. Add the onion and cook over a medium heat for 10 minutes until soft and golden. Add the garlic, cook for 1 minute, then add the butter beans and spinach. Cook for 1–2 minutes to warm through and wilt the spinach.

2 Meanwhile, brush the lamb chops with a little oil, and fry in a separate pan for 3–4 minutes on each side.

3 To make the dressing, put the olive oil, yogurt, tahini, harissa and lemon juice in a bowl, and add 2 tbsp cold water. Season well with salt and pepper, and whisk everything together.

4 To serve, divide the butter bean mixture among four warmed plates. Top with the lamb chops, add a dollop of dressing and serve with lemon wedges to squeeze over.

Serves 4	EASY		NUTRITIONAL INFORMATION	
	Preparation Time 5 minutes	**Cooking Time** 12–13 minutes	**Per Serving** 489 calories, 25g fat (of which 8g saturates), 29g carbohydrate, 2.1g salt	Gluten free

700g (1½lb) rump or fillet steak, trimmed

50g (2oz) unsalted butter or 4 tbsp olive oil

1 onion, thinly sliced

225g (8oz) brown-cap mushrooms, sliced

3 tbsp brandy

1 tsp French mustard

200ml (7fl oz) crème fraîche

100ml (3½fl oz) double cream

3 tbsp freshly chopped flat-leafed parsley

salt and ground black pepper

rice or noodles to serve

Beef Stroganoff

1 Cut the steak into strips about 5mm (¼in) wide and 5cm (2in) long.

2 Heat half the butter or olive oil in a large heavy frying pan over a medium heat. Add the onion and cook gently for 10 minutes or until soft and golden; remove with a slotted spoon and put to one side. Add the mushrooms to the pan and cook, stirring, for 2–3 minutes until golden brown; remove and put to one side.

3 Increase the heat and quickly fry the meat, in two or three batches, for 2–3 minutes, stirring constantly to ensure even browning. Add the brandy and let bubble to reduce.

4 Put all the meat, onion and mushrooms back in the pan. Reduce the heat, and stir in the mustard, crème fraîche and cream. Heat through, stir in most of the parsley and season with salt and pepper. Serve with rice or noodles, with the remaining parsley scattered over the top.

EASY		NUTRITIONAL INFORMATION		Serves
Preparation Time 10 minutes	**Cooking Time** about 20 minutes	**Per Serving** 750 calories, 60g fat (of which 35g saturates), 3g carbohydrate, 0.5g salt	Gluten free	**4**

5

Quick and Easy Puddings

Cheat's Raspberry Ice Cream

300g (11oz) frozen raspberries
5–6 tbsp golden icing sugar
300ml (½ pint) extra-thick double cream
summer fruit or wafers to serve

1 Put six ramekins or freezerproof glasses into the freezer to chill. Put the frozen raspberries (don't allow them to thaw first) into a food processor with the icing sugar. Whiz for 3–4 seconds until the raspberries look like large crumbs. Add the cream and whiz again for 10 seconds.

2 Spoon into the ice-cold dishes and serve immediately, or spoon into a small freezerproof container and freeze for 20–30 minutes. Serve with summer fruit or wafers, if you like.

Cook's Tip

Depending on the sweetness of the raspberries, you may need to add a little more icing sugar – taste the mixture before you spoon the ice cream into the dishes.

EASY

Preparation Time
5 minutes

NUTRITIONAL INFORMATION

Per Serving
306 calories, 26g fat (of which 16g saturates),
19g carbohydrate, 0g salt

Vegetarian
Gluten free

Serves
6

Fruity Fool

500g carton summer fruit compote

500g carton fresh custard sauce

1 Divide half the compote among six serving glasses, then add a thin layer of custard sauce. Repeat the process until all the compote and custard has been used.

2 Stir each fool once to swirl the custard and compote together, then serve.

Serves 6	EASY	NUTRITIONAL INFORMATION	
	Preparation Time 1–2 minutes	**Per Serving** 159 calories, 2g fat (of which 0g saturates), 31g carbohydrate, 0.1g salt	Vegetarian Gluten free

Quick Lemon Mousse

6 tbsp lemon curd

300ml ($\frac{1}{2}$ pint) double cream, whipped

fresh blueberries to decorate

1 Gently stir the lemon curd through the double cream until combined, and decorate with blueberries.

EASY	NUTRITIONAL INFORMATION		Serves
Preparation Time 1–2 minutes	**Per Serving** 334 calories, 30g fat (of which 18g saturates), 16g carbohydrate, 0.1g salt	Vegetarian Gluten free	**4**

Cherry Yogurt Crush

400g can stoned cherries, drained, or 450g (1lb) fresh
cherries, stoned

500g (1lb 2oz) Greek yogurt

150g (5oz) ratafia biscuits

4 tbsp cherry brandy (optional)

1 Spoon some cherries into the base of each of four 400ml (14fl oz) serving glasses. Top with a dollop of yogurt, some ratafia biscuits and a drizzle of cherry brandy if you like. Continue layering up each glass until all the ingredients have been used.

2 Chill for 15 minutes–2 hours before serving.

Serves	EASY	NUTRITIONAL INFORMATION	
4	**Preparation Time** 10 minutes, plus chilling	**Per Serving** 390 calories, 18g fat (of which 9g saturates), 45g carbohydrate, 0.5g salt	Vegetarian

Sticky Maple Syrup Pineapple

1 large fresh pineapple

200ml (7fl oz) maple syrup

1 Peel the pineapple and cut lengthways into quarters. Cut away the central woody core from each pineapple quarter. Slice each one lengthways into four to make 16 wedges.

2 Pour the maple syrup into a large non-stick frying pan and heat for 2 minutes. Add the pineapple and fry for 3 minutes, turning once, until warmed through.

3 Divide the pineapple among four serving plates, drizzle the maple syrup over and around the pineapple, and serve immediately.

Serves 4	EASY		NUTRITIONAL INFORMATION	
	Preparation Time 15 minutes	**Cooking Time** 5 minutes	**Per Serving** 231 calories, trace fat, 60g carbohydrate, 0.3g salt	Vegetarian Gluten free • Dairy free

▶ **Kerala Fish Curry** (see page 96)
▽ **Golden Honey Fruits**

Golden Honey Fruits

900g (2lb) selection of tropical fruit, such as pineapple, mango, papaya and banana

3 tbsp runny honey

Greek yogurt to serve

mixed spice to sprinkle

1 Preheat the grill to high. Peel the fruit as necessary, and cut into wedges.

2 Put the fruit on a foil-lined grill pan, drizzle with the honey and cook under the grill for 5–8 minutes until caramelised.

3 Serve with the yogurt, sprinkled with a little mixed spice.

EASY		NUTRITIONAL INFORMATION		Serves
Preparation Time 5 minutes	**Cooking Time** 5–8 minutes	**Per Serving** 160 calories, trace fat, 40g carbohydrate, 0g salt	Vegetarian Gluten free	**4**

Strawberry and Chocolate Muffins

2 chocolate muffins, halved

4 tbsp mascarpone cheese, softened

600g (1lb 5oz) strawberries, hulled and roughly chopped

plain chocolate (at least 70% cocoa solids), grated, to decorate

1 Divide the muffin halves among four plates. Top each half with a tablespoon of the mascarpone and a good spoonful of strawberries.

2 Sprinkle with the grated chocolate, and serve immediately.

Serves 4	EASY		NUTRITIONAL INFORMATION	
	Preparation Time 5 minutes		**Per Serving** 420 calories, 20g fat (of which 12g saturates), 55g carbohydrate, 0.6g salt	Vegetarian

2 large eggs

150ml (¼ pint) milk

finely grated zest of 1 orange

50g (2oz) butter

8 slices raisin bread, halved diagonally

1 tbsp caster sugar

vanilla ice cream and orange segments to serve (optional)

Orange Eggy Bread

1 Lightly whisk the eggs, milk and orange zest together in a bowl.

2 Heat the butter in a large frying pan over a medium heat. Dip the slices of raisin bread into the egg mixture, and fry on both sides until golden.

3 Sprinkle the bread with the sugar, and serve immediately with ice cream and orange slices if you like.

EASY		NUTRITIONAL INFORMATION		Serves
Preparation Time 10 minutes	**Cooking Time** 15 minutes	**Per Serving** 358 calories, 13g fat (of which 7g saturates), 54g carbohydrate, 1.2g salt	Vegetarian	**4**

Zabaglione

4 medium egg yolks

100g (3½oz) caster sugar

100ml (3½fl oz) sweet Marsala

1 Heat a pan of water to boiling point. Put the egg yolks and sugar into a heatproof bowl large enough to rest over the pan without touching the base. With the bowl in place, reduce the heat so that the water is just simmering.

2 Using a hand-held mixer, whisk the yolks and sugar for 15 minutes until pale, thick and foaming. With the bowl still over the heat, gradually pour in the Marsala, whisking all the time.

3 Pour the zabaglione into four glasses or small coffee cups, and serve immediately.

Serves 4	EASY		NUTRITIONAL INFORMATION	
	Preparation Time 5 minutes	**Cooking Time** 20 minutes	**Per Serving** 193 calories, 6g fat (of which 2g saturates), 28g carbohydrate, 0g salt	Vegetarian Gluten free • Dairy free

Marinated Strawberries

350g (12oz) strawberries
juice of ½ lemon
2 tbsp golden caster sugar
vanilla ice cream to serve

1 Hull the strawberries and cut in half, if large. Put in a bowl with the lemon juice and caster sugar. Stir to mix, then put to one side for 30 minutes.

2 Serve with scoops of vanilla ice cream.

EASY	NUTRITIONAL INFORMATION		Serves
Preparation Time 5 minutes, plus 30 minutes marinating	**Per Serving, without ice cream** 47 calories, trace fat, 12g carbohydrate, 0g salt	Vegetarian Gluten free	**4**

Rich Chocolate Pots

300g bar chocolate-flavour cake covering

300g (11oz) plain chocolate (at least 70% cocoa solids), broken into chunks

300ml (½ pint) double cream

250g (9oz) mascarpone

3 tbsp Cognac

1 tbsp vanilla extract

6 tbsp crème fraîche

1 Put the cake covering on a board and, using a very sharp knife, scrape against it to make 12 curls. (Use a vegetable peeler if you find it easier.) Chill until needed.

2 Melt the plain chocolate in a heatproof bowl over a pan of gently simmering water, making sure the base of the bowl doesn't touch the water. Remove from the heat and add the cream, mascarpone, Cognac and vanilla. Mix well – the hot chocolate will melt into the cream and mascarpone.

3 Divide the mixture among six 150ml (¼ pint) glasses, and chill for 20 minutes. Spoon some crème fraîche on top of each chocolate pot, and decorate with the chocolate curls.

Get Ahead

Make the chocolate curls and keep in a sealed container in the refrigerator for up to one day.

EASY		NUTRITIONAL INFORMATION		Serves
Preparation Time 10 minutes, plus 20 minutes chilling	**Cooking Time** 10 minutes	**Per Serving** 895 calories, 66g fat (of which 41g saturates), 66g carbohydrate, 0g salt	Vegetarian Gluten free	**6**

Cook's Tip

To prepare the strips of zest, pare the rind from the lemon, remove any white pith, and finely slice the zest into long strips.

If you're short of time, buy a packet of crystallised lemon slices and use these to decorate the pudding. Alternatively, decorate each biscuit with a little finely grated lemon zest.

Amaretti with Lemon Mascarpone

finely sliced zest and juice of ¼ lemon (see Cook's Tips)
1 tbsp golden caster sugar, plus a little extra to sprinkle
50g (2oz) mascarpone
12 single amaretti biscuits

1 Put the lemon juice in a small pan. Add the sugar and dissolve over a low heat. Once the sugar has dissolved, add the lemon zest and cook for 1–2 minutes – it will curl up. Lift out the zest strips using a slotted spoon, and lay on a sheet of baking parchment, reserving the syrup. Sprinkle the strips with sugar to coat.

2 Beat the mascarpone in a bowl to soften, then stir in the reserved sugar syrup.

3 Put a blob of mascarpone on each amaretti biscuit, then top with a couple of strips of the crystallised lemon peel.

Serves 4	EASY		NUTRITIONAL INFORMATION	
	Preparation Time 15 minutes	**Cooking Time** 5 minutes	**Per Serving** 180 calories, 8g fat (of which 4g saturates), 28g carbohydrate, 0.4g salt	Vegetarian

Glossary

Al dente Italian term commonly used to describe foods, especially pasta and vegetables, which are cooked until tender but still firm to the bite.

Baking blind Pre-baking a pastry case before filling. The pastry case is lined with greaseproof paper and weighted down with dried beans or ceramic baking beans.

Baste To spoon the juices and melted fat over meat, poultry, game or vegetables during roasting to keep them moist. The term is also used to describe spooning over a marinade.

Beat To incorporate air into an ingredient or mixture by agitating it vigorously with a spoon, fork, whisk or electric mixer. The technique is also used to soften ingredients.

Bind To mix beaten egg or other liquid into a dry mixture to hold it together.

Blanch To immerse food briefly in fast-boiling water to loosen skins, such as peaches or tomatoes, or to remove bitterness, or to destroy enzymes and preserve the colour, flavour and texture of vegetables (especially prior to freezing).

Bouquet garni Small bunch of herbs – usually a mixture of parsley stems, thyme and a bay leaf – tied in muslin and used to flavour stocks, soups and stews.

Braise To cook meat, poultry, game or vegetables slowly in a small amount of liquid in a pan or casserole with a tight-fitting lid. The food is usually first browned in oil or fat.

Caramelise To heat sugar or sugar syrup slowly until it is brown in colour; ie forms a caramel.

Chill To cool food in the fridge.

Compote Fresh or dried fruit stewed in sugar syrup. Served hot or cold.

Coulis A smooth fruit or vegetable purée, thinned if necessary to a pouring consistency.

Cream To beat together fat and sugar until the mixture is pale and fluffy, and resembles whipped cream in texture and colour. The method is used in cakes and puddings which contain a high proportion of fat and require the incorporation of a lot of air.

Croûtons Small pieces of fried or toasted bread, served with soups and salads.

Crudités Raw vegetables, usually cut into slices or sticks, typically served with a dipping sauce.

Curdle To cause sauces or creamed mixtures to separate, usually by overheating or over-beating.

Cure To preserve fish, meat or poultry by smoking, drying or salting.

Deglaze To heat stock, wine or other liquid with the cooking juices left in the pan after roasting or sautéeing, scraping and stirring vigorously to dissolve the sediment on the bottom of the pan.

Dice To cut food into small cubes.

Dredge To sprinkle food generously with flour, sugar, icing sugar etc.

Dust To sprinkle lightly with flour, cornflour, icing sugar etc.

Escalope Thin slice of meat, such as pork, veal or turkey, from the top of the leg, usually pan-fried.

Fillet Term used to describe boned breasts of birds, boned sides of fish, and the undercut of a loin of beef, lamb, pork or veal.

Flake To separate food, such as cooked fish, into natural pieces.

Folding in Method of combining a whisked or creamed mixture with other ingredients by cutting and folding so that it retains its lightness. A large metal spoon or plastic-bladed spatula is used.

Fry To cook food in hot fat or oil. There are various methods: shallow-frying in a little fat in a shallow pan; deep-frying where the food is totally immersed in oil; dry-frying in which fatty foods are cooked in a non-stick pan without extra fat; see also Stir-frying.

Garnish A decoration, usually edible, such as parsley or lemon, which is used to enhance the appearance of a savoury dish.

Gluten A protein constituent of grains, such as wheat and rye, which develops when the flour is mixed with water to give the dough elasticity.

Griddle A flat, heavy, metal plate used on the hob for cooking scones or for searing savoury ingredients.

Gut To clean out the entrails from fish.

Hull To remove the stalk and calyx from soft fruits, such as strawberries.

Infuse To immerse flavourings, such as aromatic vegetables, herbs, spices and vanilla, in a liquid to impart flavour. Usually the infused liquid is brought to the boil, then left to stand for a while.

Julienne Fine 'matchstick' strips of vegetables or citrus zest, sometimes used as a garnish.

Macerate To soften and flavour raw or dried foods by soaking in a liquid, eg soaking fruit in alcohol.

Marinate To soak raw meat, poultry or game – usually in a mixture of oil, wine, vinegar and flavourings – to soften and impart flavour. The mixture, which is known as a marinade, may also be used to baste the food during cooking.

Medallion Small round piece of meat, usually beef or veal.

Mince To cut food into very fine pieces, using a mincer, food processor or knife.

Parboil To boil a vegetable or other food for part of its cooking time before finishing it by another method.

Pare To finely peel the skin or zest from vegetables or fruit.

Poach To cook food gently in liquid at simmering point; the surface should be just trembling.

Pot roast To cook meat in a covered pan with some fat and a little liquid.

Purée To pound, sieve or liquidise vegetables, fish or fruit to a smooth pulp. Purées often form the basis for soups and sauces.

Reduce To fast-boil stock or other liquid in an uncovered pan to evaporate water and concentrate the flavour.

Refresh To cool hot vegetables very quickly by plunging into ice-cold water or holding under cold running water in order to stop the cooking process and preserve the colour.

Roast To cook food by dry heat in the oven.

Roux A mixture of equal quantities of butter (or other fat) and flour cooked together to form the basis of many sauces.

Rubbing in Method of incorporating fat into flour by rubbing between the fingertips, used when a short texture is required. Used for pastry, cakes, scones and biscuits.

Salsa Piquant sauce made from chopped fresh vegetables and sometimes fruit.

Sauté To cook food in a small quantity of fat over a high heat, shaking the pan constantly – usually in a sauté pan (a frying pan with straight sides and a wide base).

Scald To pour boiling water over food to clean it, or loosen skin, eg tomatoes. Also used to describe heating milk to just below boiling point.

Score To cut parallel lines in the surface of food, such as fish (or the fat layer on meat), to improve its appearance or help it cook more quickly.

Sear To brown meat quickly in a little hot fat before grilling or roasting.

Seasoned flour Flour mixed with a little salt and pepper, used for dusting meat, fish etc., before frying.

Shred To grate cheese or slice vegetables into very fine pieces or strips.

Sieve To press food through a perforated sieve to obtain a smooth texture.

Sift To shake dry ingredients through a sieve to remove lumps.

Simmer To keep a liquid just below boiling point.

Skim To remove froth, scum or fat from the surface of stock, gravy, stews, jam etc. Use either a skimmer, a spoon or kitchen paper.

Steam To cook food in steam, usually in a steamer over rapidly boiling water.

Steep To immerse food in warm or cold liquid to soften it, and sometimes to draw out strong flavours.

Stew To cook food, such as tougher cuts of meat, in flavoured liquid which is kept at simmering point.

Stir-fry To cook small even-sized pieces of food rapidly in a little fat, tossing constantly over a high heat.

Sweat To cook chopped or sliced vegetables in a little fat without liquid in a covered pan over a low heat to soften.

Tepid The term used to describe temperature at approximately blood heat, ie 37°C (98.7°F).

Vanilla sugar Sugar in which a vanilla pod has been stored to impart its flavour.

Whipping (whisking) Beating air rapidly into a mixture either with a manual or electric whisk. Whipping usually refers to cream.

Zest The thin coloured outer layer of citrus fruit, which can be removed in fine strips with a zester.

Index